GIVING AWAY
THE TRICK

GIVING AWAY THE TRICK

HOW WE DO ALL THAT STUFF WITH COMPUTERS

John J. Smith

Original Cover Art by Robert P.J. Smith

CONTENTS

PREFACE:

We're magicians you know. We do magic tricks. Not the Harry Potter kind of magic, though it seems that way sometimes. We do the Penn and Teller kind of magic. We are the kind of magicians that work out a trick behind the scenes and then bring it out to show you.

Just like sleight-of-hand, these tricks involve things that happen so fast you don't see the trick being assembled right in front of your eyes.

All you get to see are the results.

But it's all tricks - really cool, really useful tricks, - but they're tricks.

And just like every cool trick you ever saw some magician do, there is an explanation on how they did it, and it's not as complicated as most people think, not the least bit mysterious, and not even all that difficult to understand.

So - do you want to know how the tricks are done?

INTRODUCTION:

You may have noticed that we can do a lot of different things with computers, unbelievably different things. We use them to keep time and to control airplanes and spaceships. We use them to do our taxes and save medical records. We use them to give us answers in plain spoken language, and to put persons, places, and things straight out of our imaginations onto movie screens. We even use them to pump our brakes to stop on snowy roads.

And yet, computers are not built to do any of those things. Computers are tools. They are simple basic tools that do simple basic stuff. They are tools to build stuff with. Just like when you take a saw and a hammer - tools that are built to cut wood and hammer nails - and use them to turn raw materials into elaborate structures, computers can be used to build all kinds of things by using the simple functions that they do.

A blank piece of paper, or an empty canvas, stays empty until someone with an idea writes something, or paints something. A computer is just like a blank piece of paper or an empty canvas, it does nothing until a person gives it instructions, and just like the blank piece of paper or the empty canvas where there are no rules or guidelines on what can be written or painted, what you can do on a computer is open-ended, a computer can do whatever someone can think of to instruct it to do.

PART ONE:
BINARY DIGITAL

Section 1: What is Digital Anyway?

We're humans, we like to tell each other stuff. We even like to tell each other stuff when we're away from each other. So, humans have invented ways to send other humans messages.

Most of it was sending words by sending words. A messenger would memorize a message and run five miles to tell it to someone, or a message gets written down and the messenger runs five miles to hand it to someone.

But there are other ways to send messages that humans have come up with and one way is with numbers. Sending a few numbers makes it much easier to send messages over long distances or to large groups of people.

Think about things like jungle drums, or smoke signals, or military bugles, or lanterns in towers. What these methods of communication all have in common is that they use numbers to send messages. The numbers are in the form of how many things there are, or a rhythmic pattern, or a sequence of notes.

Of course, when you send messages this way the person receiving it has to know ahead of time what the numbers mean. You can think of this as a very simple code where each number sends a whole complete message.

Take for example the Paul Revere warning system, which was based on the lantern count in a tower in the night:

if **Lantern count** = 0 then **'message pending'**
if **Lantern count** = 1 then **'British by land'**
if **Lantern count** = 2 then **'British by sea'**

This as a type of digital communications. Of course when we talk about digital what we are really talking about is what goes on inside our digital devices - our computers and phones - and what goes on inside our computers and phones is even simpler than the Paul Revere system, because instead of using three digits: 0, 1, and 2 for the messages, we only use two: 0 and 1.

This is not done by sending the actual numbers 0 and 1, it is even more basic and simpler than that – it is done by sending two different things and just calling one '1' and the other one '0'.

It's a great trick, you can even think of this as the fundamental trick of digital electronics: that it is all done by using only 2 different signals, one is called 'zero' and one is called 'one' and they are put into patterns to create all kinds of things, in fact these two things give us everything.

Section 2: Dots, Dashes, Zeros, and Ones

With digital electronics, the signals come one after another at perfectly timed intervals, they are called bits, and they can only be one of only two different things.

It does not matter what the two different things are just as long as they are different enough to tell one from the other.

Why two things?

One is not enough. If you only had one thing all you can send is that one thing over and over again. But with just two things, if you can line them up in order, then you can arrange them in all kinds of patterns, which lets you send all kinds of messages.

So, with a clever use of simple patterns, by arranging only two different things in many different ways, you can send many different patterns, which gives you many different numbers, and therefore many different number-based messages.

In fact, with just these two different things we can create enough patterns to create enough different numbers to do everything we do digitally.

EVERYTHING.

How? Think Morse Code. Dashes and dots. The first telegraph.

A person on one end of a wire sits and reads characters from a slip of paper and taps combinations of long and short taps on a button to represent the characters. On the other end of the wire sits another person who listens to the patterns of long and short clicks and translates them into characters and writes them down on another piece of paper.

This is an early example of digital communications, the kind of thing we do with digital devices, it is using two different signals to send messages.

It does not matter that we call the two different things dash and dot instead of zero and one. It really is the same thing. It is sending two different types of electrical pulses through a wire that we treat as two different things.

Which is exactly how digital communications work - patterns of two different signals are sent through wires, fiber optics, or the airways (wireless) with the simple requirement that there are two things that you can tell one from the other.

The two different things used in Morse code are the dash and dot, which is just what they call a long and short signal. The dashes and dots come from holding the button down longer or shorter, which makes the electrical signal longer and shorter. It would probably be more descriptive to call the two different things long and short, but they are called dash and dot.

For digital electronics, instead of using short and long, they use big and small - as in the number of volts. It does not matter how many volts are used for the two different signals, just as long as there are only two and they are different enough to tell them apart.

Of course, just having two different things is not going to get you much, they have to be used in combination with each other to do anything. That's what happens in Morse code when they combine the dashes and dots to stand for letters of the alphabet.

This is exactly what we do in digital electronics, the two things are combined into patterns in order to do things, in fact it is this combining of two different signals into patterns that gives us everything.

I want to pound this point home a little: *by using patterns of only two different things we get everything we do from digital electronics* - everything from CGI to artificial intelligence.

So how can patterns of just two different things give us all that stuff?

Once again let's look at Morse Code. As you know, Morse Code only has two things: dot and dash, which are transmitted by sending short and long signals, and yet the entire alphabet is built with combinations of these short and long taps.

Everything that can be spelled with letters of the alphabet can be sent using Morse Code. Given enough time and a very strong, extremely durable finger, a telegraph operator could send the entire works of Shakespeare, or the novel War and Peace across a wire all with just dots and dashes.

With digital electronics, it's an electronic circuit that is doing the work - which is much faster than a human's finger, but just like the telegraph operator, all it sends are patterns of just two different signals - lower and higher voltage signals.

So, what is the difference between a man tapping out dots and dashes and digital electronics tapping out zeros and ones?

Conceptually, Not much.

Why can we do so much more with electronics?

The answer is simple: speed.

Humans can only hit the switch at human speeds, but electronics have that whole 'near-light-speed' thing going for them and can flip the switch absurdly fast. With a human expert doing Morse Code the rate might be three or four times a second, with electronics the switches can be flipped millions, or even billions of times per second.

Giving Away the Trick

To understand the difference speed makes - picture that guy that types out characters on one of those old telegraph machines you might have seen in the movies. He would have to tap that thing 9,600 times a second just to be as fast as the old (painfully slow) dial-up connections they used back in the ancient times of the 1990s.

You've heard the commercials for gigabit speeds? - well, at a gigabit per second that poor person would have to click that telegraph thing over a billion times a second.

That's billion with a 'B'.

Now that's really, *really* fast Morse Code.

The other difference between Morse Code and digital electronics is how we use the two different things we send over the wire. In Morse Code the two different signals are called dot and dash and are just used to create patterns that are assigned to letters of the alphabet.

In digital electronics we also do the Morse code thing of assigning patterns to letters of the alphabet, but the two different things that we call zero and one are not just referred to as zero and one, we actually use them as the mathematical numbers zero and one, which, as I will explain, lets us do all the other things we do beyond just sending messages.

There is one other important difference. With Morse code the operator pauses slightly between each letter to indicate where one letter ends and the other one begins, but with digital electronics the signals come perfectly timed one after another without stopping or pausing, this allows the electronics to use time to keep track of every single zero and one.

By the way, making the two different things be zero and one can be done with Morse code. A dot could be called 'zero' and a dash could be called 'one', so instead of SOS being dot dot dot dash dash dash dot dot dot it would be 0 0 0   1 1 1   0 0 0.

Section 3: Everything with Zeros and Ones

I guess there needs to be a quick lesson in binary.

Binary which means 'system of two' is a number system that uses two digits, the same way that decimal is a number system that uses ten digits.

For us humans, we think in decimal. It is so much a part of us that it's hard to picture any other way to count but in tens. But really the only reason that counting in tens is so natural for us, is that we evolved to have ten fingers to count on.

From a mathematical point-of-view it would be so much simpler to count in eights instead of tens. If we all evolved to have only 4 fingers per hand like in the Simpsons our world would be a much simpler place mathematically.

But because of our freakish five-fingers hands, other number systems seem weird, and binary seems especially weird and unnatural. Think of it as just numbers, the same numbers as always - just a different way of representing them.

This is how it works:

In decimal there are the ten digits we all know and love: 0 through 9.

When we count, we start with one digit and roll through all the values, 1, 2, 3, 4,... until we hit the last value 9, and then to go to the next value which we use 2 digits to represent so we go to 10, and then roll through all the values that a 2 digit number can be 10, 11, 12, ..., 34, 35, 36, ..., 97, 98, and then we hit 99 and have go to three digits so we go to 100, and so on.

In binary we only have two values 0 and 1, so when we count in binary we run out of single-digit values right away at 1 and have to go to the first two-digit number which is 10 and then we run out of two-digit numbers at 11 instead of 99, and we have to go to the first three-digit number which is 100.

By the way, for those of you that want to speak correctly in binary, the number 10 is not 'ten', and 100 is not 'one hundred'. In binary '10' is pronounced 'one zero' and '100' is pronounced 'one zero zero'.

Now here's the really cool part (assuming that you think anything related to numbers is cool) - binary math works the same as decimal math. The only difference is how we represent the numbers. So even though in binary $1 + 1 = 10$, in terms of the actual mathematical value - one plus one still always equals two, it's just that two in binary is written as '10' ('one zero').

Don't worry if you can't work in binary, I have to admit that being one of those 5-fingers-per-hand humans, it really took me a while to get used to working with it. To begin with, there are just way too many digits to deal with, after all, 8 is a four-digit number in binary.

Probably the most annoying part of working in binary is how much carrying you have to do when adding. Just adding 1 plus 1 results in a carry: "one plus one is zero, carry one...". So yeah, it's a bit weird.

But I want to run through a little bit of binary math.

In Binary, the same as decimal, one plus one equals two, but it is written:

$1 + 1 = 10$

and two plus one equals three, but it is written:

$10 + 1 = 11$

because in binary two is 10 and a binary three is 11.

taking it one step further - In binary, three plus one equals four and that is written:

$11 + 1 = 100$

Hopefully you are noticing the rather simple pattern.

The point is that by using zero and one as the only values for the digits, and having enough places, we can keep counting up to represent every integer in binary, all infinity of them.

Decimal		Binary
0	=	0
1	=	1
2	=	10
3	=	11
4	=	100
5	=	101
6	=	110
7	=	111
8	=	1000
9	=	1001
10	=	1010
11	=	1011
12	=	1100
13	=	1101
14	=	1110
15	=	1111
16	=	10000
32	=	100000
64	=	1000000
128	=	10000000
256	=	100000000
512	=	1000000000
1024	=	10000000000

As you can see, the numbers go up fast every time you add another place for another digit, in fact they double, so that with only 8 places, you can represent every integer from 0 to 255, and with 16 places, every number from 0 to 65,535 can be represented.

This is probably a good time to start to use the term 'bit' instead of 'places'. It is short for 'binary digit' and it's the equivalent of 'decimal place' for binary numbers, and when talking about digital anything, it is used a lot.

With 32 bits you can represent every integer from 0 to 4,294,967,295.

If you have enough places for zeros and ones, you can count as high as you want, which comes in very handy when trying to represent things in the real world with a unique number.

For example, if you had two things such as yes or no, or right or left, all you would need is a single bit: 1 = yes, 0 = no, 1 = right, 0 = left. If it was four things such as Spades, Hearts, Clubs, or Diamonds it would take two bits to cover all four: 00 = Spades, 01 = Hearts, 10 = Clubs, 11 = Diamonds.

So, no matter how many things there are in a list to assign IDs to, all you need is enough bits to cover it. If you wanted a unique ID number for all the people in China, you could do it with 32 bits.

And it goes way beyond counting. The really great thing is that by using zero and one - actual mathematical numbers - and combining them to be all the other numbers, **all** of the regular math will work with those numbers. Addition, subtraction, multiplication, division, algebra, geometry, even calculus, all work in binary the same as in decimal.

So, with just zeros and ones, you can have all the integers, and all of the math. So, if all you are working with is numbers and all you are doing with those numbers is math you can do it all in binary.

Of course, everybody knows that digital computers don't just work with numbers, they work with things that are not numbers, like text, pictures, sound, even video and speech...

[cue suspense music] ...

or do they????

Nah, not really - they just work with numbers.

Section 4: Representing the world in numbers

Humans have been using numbers to represent things for centuries. ID numbers and measurements are just some of the ways we represent non-numbers as numbers. A great deal of science is involved in turning physical phenomena into numbers and then doing math with those numbers to figure other stuff out.

Just about anything we work with can be described with numbers, and with enough places for zeros and ones any size number can be represented. So, the way that we deal with everything that isn't a number is to turn whatever it is into numbers. This can be done by assigning, listing, counting, or measuring. Then once something is represented by numbers, we can then work with the numbers.

For example, if it's text you need, then what you do is simply assign a unique number to each character in the language.

You don't even need that many places to do it.

For the entire English language we only need 8 bits, which gives us 256 unique numbers, which is more than enough to assign a unique number to all 26 lower case letters, plus the 26 upper case letters, plus the 10 numerical digits, plus all the punctuation, and also a bunch of special symbols, and there are even a few spare numbers to assign something to whatever we want to.

By the way, the reason that computers are case sensitive is that the assigned numbers for lower-case letters are different that the assigned numbers for upper-case letters. 'a' does not equal 'A'.

Chinese, with tens of thousands of characters, can be covered with 16-place binary numbers.

I really do mean that the number value for letters are assigned. Which number represents which character in a language is completely arbitrary. Over the years different people in different companies and countries have assigned totally different numbers to the different characters in the different languages.

That's how text is done, what about pictures?

A digital picture is not a picture, not in how we think of pictures. A digital picture is a list of numbers. Yes numbers - and those numbers are made up of bits, you know, zeros and ones.

Each number represents a color, the more bits that are used per color, the more colors and shades of colors there can be.

For example, the original color card for an IBM PC used 4-bit colors - which gives you a whopping 16 different colors. To say the least, computers have become more colorful, you might have heard absurd numbers like 'over 4 billion colors', what that means is that they are almost certainly using 32 bits for the color numbers for each color dot on the screen.

The tiny dots of colors I mentioned are the pixels you may have heard of. The more pixels there are in a picture, the smaller the pixels have to be to fit on the screen, and if the pixels are small enough it becomes almost impossible to see where one pixel ends and the next one begins, and the picture on the screen looks like a smooth continuous picture. That's why it's better to have more pixels (measured in megapixels - a million pixels) with a digital camera.

The point is - it's is all just numbers. Text is numbers, pictures are numbers, sound - yep - numbers. A digital computer only works with numbers, - numbers made up of zeros and ones.

I know I am being a bit repetitious here but this is very important to understanding how we do things with digital computers - that simple zeros and ones are combined to be numbers and those numbers are used to represent everything we do with digital technology including: characters in a book, colors in a picture, people in the company, vibrations in a sound, position in space, stars in the sky, etc.

The expression - 'it's all just zeros and ones' is absolutely true, because it *is* all just zeros and ones.

John J. Smith

PART TWO: THE PROCESSOR

Section 1: Bits

Let's talk about bits.

Everything in digital technology involves zeros and ones. There are zeros and ones everywhere and there are lots of them, usually counted in the millions or billions, sometimes even in trillions. But here's the thing - there is no one place for the zeros and another place for the ones. You cannot point at something and say that's where all the ones are or where the zeros are. In fact the thing that makes digital technology so useful is that most of the things that can be zeros can also be ones and vice versa.

That's where the term 'bits' comes in. The term bits, which is short for 'binary digit' is the same as the term 'decimal places' except that it's for binary numbers - in other words - it's the position of a binary digit in a binary number. But the way bits is used when talking about digital technology goes way beyond just a position in a number. Just about anything that can be either a zero or a one is considered a bit, provided it is in a row of other identical things that can also be zero or one. It doesn't matter if it's a concept, an abstraction, or an actual physical thing - if it can be either a zero or a one, and it's in a row of other things that can be either zero or one - it's a bit.

Bits can be signals going through wires, light pulses through fiber optic cables, electric cells in computer memory, the holes punched out of a punch card, switches in a circuit, marks on a paper, locations on a disk drive, etc.

So as I talk about bits - and I *will* talk about bits - I am hoping that it will be less confusing if you think of a bit as anything that can be either a zero or one in a row of things that can be either zero or one, regardless of whether it's conceptual, an abstraction, or a physical thing.

The reason why it is important to understand bits this way is that with digital computers - that's all there is. Really. The only things that digital electronics work with are the 'bits'.

Inside digital computers bits are changed from zero to one and one to zero, they are copied, added, subtracted, compared, stored, and transmitted, they have logic operations performed on them, and even the very operations that are performed on bits are done based on instructions that are themselves patterns of bits.

Basically, in a computer, bits are processed, and the thing inside a computer that processes the bits has the ridiculously appropriate name - the processor.

Section 2: Not the Brain

Sometimes how we talk about things can create an image in our minds that is completely wrong. A good example of that is when the processor is referred to as the 'brain' of the computer. This could be one of the most misleading and completely wrong analogies in history, as there is nothing in a computer that is close to being like a brain. Just because we can make them *seem to act* like a brain, does not mean they actually function like a brain. Saying a processor is the brain of a computer is no less off the mark than saying the headlights are the eyes of a car.

A processor does not function like a brain, - not even close. It does not think, know, learn, or understand. All a processor does are a limited number of operations that it performs on patterns of bits, and the kind of operations processors do on the bits are actually quite simple. I think most people would be quite surprised by just how simple the operations a processor does are.

Even more un-brain-like, a processor only does one of these simple operations at a time.

And what is the processor doing to the bit patterns when it processes them one-at-a-time?

Well, bits can only be either zero or one, so basically all a processor does is turn the bits in a pattern to either zero or one. That's it - all digital computing is done by having processors turn bits in bit patterns to either zero or one, there really is nothing more than that.

Really, I swear.

Of course, the bits are not turned on or off at random, but in specific ways depending on what the operation the processor is instructed to do and the kind of operations the processor does with these bit patterns are just simple logic and simple arithmetic, and some simple direct manipulation of the bits.

They do things like adding, subtracting, and comparing. They do logic operations such as 'and', 'not', 'or' and 'exclusive or', and they do things like changing specific bits to zero or one, or shifting the value in one bit to the bit next to it, or copying whole patterns of bits from one set of bits in one location to another.

Processors, like everything digital, *only* work with bit patterns made up of zeros and ones. Everything that goes into a processor is made up of zeros and ones, everything that comes out of a processor is made up of zeros and ones, and every result that comes from a processor operation is made up of zeros and ones.

And because patterns of zeros and ones are actually binary numbers, - it is also true that processors only work with numbers. So, don't think of a processor as a brain but just a device where numbers go in, numbers get manipulated, and numbers come out, no characters, no pictures, no thoughts, just numbers.

You might have heard that what processors do is execute instructions, which may sound like doing more than manipulating numbers, but a processor instruction is like every other thing in processors - it is just a number made up of zeros and ones, and all the instructions do is instruct a processor to manipulate numbers made up of zeros and ones.

A processor basically works like a mechanical device. All the bits for the numbers used in an operation act like the buttons, and whether the bit is a zero or a one is whether the button is pushed or not, and what comes out depends on which buttons are pushed. And just like a mechanical device, if the exact same buttons are pushed, the exact same result will happen, every time, automatically, mechanically.

This would be a good point to talk a little about how processors do what they do, and don't worry, I am not going to dive into the stuff the electrical engineers have to know to build them - I just want to talk about switches.

Section 3: Switches

Yes switches, - those things that turn the electricity on and off.

Do you have any 3-way switches in your house? You toggle one of the switches and the lights go on, then you go to the other switch and toggle it and the lights go off. Then you go back to the first switch and you toggle it the opposite way from before and the lights go back on.

This is because of the way that the switches and the lights are wired. The way to toggle the switch to be on or off on depends on which way the other switch is toggled (and vice versa).

This 3-way switch arrangement is actually an example of a simple logic circuit. The switches are the bits, the direction the switch is toggled is whether the bit is a zero or a one and the lights are the result, and whether the lights are on or off is whether the result is a zero or a one.

There are 4 combinations of the switches that give the following results:

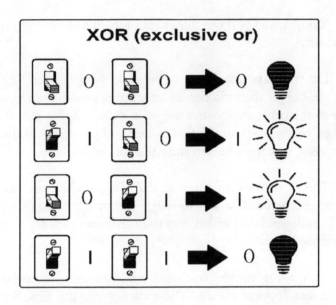

I don't know if you have ever had any exposure to logic, but this is an actual logic operation called **'exclusive or'** which means that the light bulb lights up only if one or the other switch is on, but not both.

So, let's say you wired the lights wrong and had it so that the lights only go on if both switches are turned on. This would create a different simple logic circuit. This would be the logic operation **'and'** which means that the lights are on only if switch one *and* switch two are both on (BTW: this is not the same as **'add'**).

The 4 combinations give the following results:

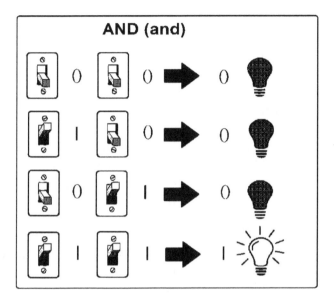

Simple logic circuits can be demonstrated by wiring switches and lightbulbs in different ways. It was not uncommon in the 1970s and 80s to go to a high school science fair and see exhibits that used household light switches and lightbulbs to demonstrate simple logic circuits used in computers.

Inside a processor there are switches, and they are wired to do these simple logic operations but of course inside a processor the switches are not household wall switches, they are electronic switches. And these switches are not 'toggled' by flipping a switch but are toggled by turning the electricity to them on and off.

But here is where it gets a bit mind-blowing to think about - the things that turn the electricity on or off to an electronic switch are other electronic switches, which, because they are electronic switches, are themselves turned on and off by other electronic switches, which are turned on and off by other electronic switches, and so on and so forth.

You don't need to get too hung up on exactly how all these switches are connected to each other - just that processors are made up of switches that switch other switches that are themselves switched by other switches.

And the simple logic circuits, which are just combinations of switches, are themselves combined with other simple logic circuits to create more complex logic circuits. Over the years as processors have gotten more sophisticated, there have been more and more complex operations built inside of them, but they are still built by combining simple logic circuits that use off-on switches that turn other off-on switches off or on.

Okay, we have finally arrived at the place where the electrical circuits become digital computers because inside the processor those switches I have been talking about... ['drum roll please'] ... are the bits!!!

Hopefully you are having an OMG moment, as in 'OMG THE SWITCHES ARE THE BITS!!!' (please don't do that exploding-mind hand gesture thing).

You see, the switches have only two possible states - on or off, which is just what is needed for binary operations - two different things. The two states (on or off) of the switches is how we use electronic circuits to create bits that have two different states which we consider to be zero and one.

That's right - all those zeros and ones you have heard about - they are the on/off state of the switches inside digital electronics.

Because processors only work with numbers, and the numbers are made up of bit patterns, and the bits in the pattern are how the switches are set, when a number is put into a processor, what that means is that a row of switches is set to the bit pattern that makes up the binary version of that number.

So basically, when you put a number into a processor what you are doing is setting a row of electronic switches to either on or off.

Just to be accurate:

The two states of the switches are not really on and off. They switch between a higher voltage signal and a lower voltage signal and that's because technically the switches are not really switches, but are these very important, totally cool, things called transistors.

The properties of transistors are very important to the electrical engineers who design microprocessors, but to understand the concepts in this book it just makes it much easier to think in terms of switches that simply turn on or off.

Section 4: Patterns of Bits

After telling you all about the wonder of bits I should point out that a single bit, which can only be zero or one, is useful only if you are dealing with only two things such as yes or no, heads or tails, up or down, - things like that. For more than two things you need more bits, and to get the most out of those bits you need to put them in order (first bit, second bit, third bit, etc.), because then you can use the different patterns of zeros and ones to be binary numbers.

A single bit can be: 0 or 1. With two bits there can be four different patterns: 00, 01, 10 or 11. Three bits gives you eight different patterns: 000, 001, 010, 011, 100, 101, 110, and 111. As you might expect, you can make 16 different patterns of zeros and ones with 4 bits and every time you add another bit, the number of possible bit patterns doubles.

This gets me into some very practical issues with the bits.

Because processors perform operations on bit patterns and not just on a single bit, it would be so much more efficient to have a processor perform operations on entire bit patterns all at once. The speed difference would be obvious – if you could process 5 bits at once it would be five times faster than doing them one-at-a-time.

How this is done is rather straightforward:

First picture a single computer logic circuit, something that manipulates one bit. Picture it as switches wired together in a particular way. Now take that single logic circuit and duplicate it as many times as the number of bits in the bit pattern you want to manipulate. Then put those duplicate circuits side-by-side in parallel so that each one manipulates one bit of the bit pattern.

This is what is done inside processors. They run parallel circuits all over the place so that all processor operations work on whole bit patterns at a time.

Which brings up the question - how many bits should a processor work on at a time? How many side-by-side, parallel circuits need to be built into a processor?

There is no natural or best answer to this. There are trade-offs and complicating factors that I won't go into here, but how many bits a processor operates on in one operation is one of the major differences between different types and generations of processors. But even though there are many differences, there are standards.

For example, somewhere along the way it was decided that the minimum most useful number of bits to operate on at one time was eight.

Eight gives you 256 different patterns of zeros and ones and it turns out that a lot of what we use computers for can be covered by 256 or less. But probably the most important are all the characters, numbers, and symbols used in the English language.

With 256 you have enough unique numbers for all upper and lower case letters, all the punctuation, the ten digits 0 through 9, and all the special characters and symbols. There are even enough for 'invisible' printing characters such as tab, blank space, line feed, and carriage return, and even some extra ones used by word processing software to do all kinds of things.

Eight bits is such a useful amount that it is used as standard unit of measurement of memory and storage space. Eight bits is called a 'byte' (pronounced 'bite') and it is used as the basic unit for counting how much space a computer has - as in bytes, kilobytes (1 thousand bytes), megabytes (1 million bytes), gigabytes (1 billion bytes), etc.

As for the actual best number of bits to operate on at one time inside a processor, that really depends on how many parallel circuits the engineers can jam into the processor. When a computer is described as having a 32 bit or a 64 bit processor, what that means is that inside the processor there are 32 or 64 side-by-side parallel circuits for each operation.

So, to clarify a point I made earlier when I said that processors only do one thing at a time, I was referring to only one operation at a time, which means the manipulation of a whole bit pattern at one time.

Section 5: Bit Twirling, Every Bit is Sacred

Bit twirling was an expression I haven't heard much lately but I thought it sounded cool, so I used it here. It used to refer to how we did a lot of what we had to do when we programmed computers that were much slower, had tiny memory by today's standards, and could store almost nothing. Bit twirling was how we did a lot of our tricks.

Today we walk around with super powerful computers in our pockets, and we forget or are too young to know how big, expensive, slow, and limited, computers used to be. Every bit that was processed or stored cost money to process and store.

For most of the early days of computers there was never enough memory, and never enough speed, and storage was slow and expensive. There was a strong economic incentive to make the data being worked on as small and efficient as possible. Every bit was precious.

We would do whatever tricks we could to use as few bits as possible, and therefore store as few characters as possible. I know I said that all that we deal with inside a processor is numbers, but that's not true all the time. The only things we actually deal with inside a processor are bits, all those zeros and ones I may have mentioned a couple of times.

Most of the time we group the bits together and treat the groups as numbers, but not all the time. Sometimes, when we were really trying to jam as much information into the smallest possible space we would directly manipulate bits in smaller groups or even as individual bits. It let us jam more information into a single byte. The technique was literally called packing.

For example, a doctor's record for someone might have a check list of yes and no questions:

- diabetes:	yes/no
- measles vaccine:	yes/no
- smoker:	yes/no
- still breathing:	yes/no

.

If we make 1 be yes and 0 be no, these could each be stored in a single bit. If there were eight yes or no questions the results could all be fit into a pattern of eight bits, or one byte. Which means you could jam eight yes/no answers in the same size bit pattern as is used for a whole single English-language character.

Think of the space savings. If you stored eight yes or no answers in single bits it would take only 8 bits to do it. If instead of using a single bit to store a 0 or a 1, you actually stored 'y' for yes and 'n', which are characters that take up 8 bits each, it would take 64 (8 x 8) bits instead of only 8 bits to save the information.

A doctor who had 1000 patients could save 56,000 bits on that one set of questions alone.

So, yeah, we packed that data in. The practice of jamming as much data into the smallest possible number of bits was fairly common because quite simply - it saved money and even space and time.

For those of you that remember floppy disks, do you remember how many floppies you ended up having to keep around, and how long it took to deal with all of them. Imagine how much worse it would have been if we weren't jamming all those bits together.

Because the processor did things in 8-bit chunks, in order to pack the data tightly you had to take a whole byte, 8 bits, and start setting the bits individually. There are all kinds operations you can do with bits and although almost no one writes code anymore to manipulate bits directly, there is still a lot of bit manipulation going on inside processor.

The Y2K problem you might have heard about was a result of the 'every bit is sacred' mentality.

Because bits were so precious, anywhere you could save space you would. You would never use numbers bigger than you had to because the bigger the number, the more bits you needed to represent it.

Giving Away the Trick

A lot of what we did involved dates, lots and lots of dates, and in the 1980s it would have been unheard of to store a date in any other format but as MMDDYY. It was not a mistake to use YY for the year instead of YYYY, it was an economic decision, based on the extra expense of using a four-digit year vs. a two-digit year. It was just assumed that by the time we got to the year 2000 we would not still be using the same programs.

What happens is that dates get compared in programs all the time. Dates are just numbers and when you compare these numbers by which is greater than or less than each other what you are really checking is if one date is before or after another date.

For example, a banking program might have code that compares today's date to the due date of a payment. If the number for today's date is greater than the number for the due date, then today is after the due date and a $30 late fee is added to the account.

So, if you are only using YY for the year and it happens to be 1999 then you are just looking at the 99. Then after stroke of midnight on January 1st, 2000, if you are only using YY for the year then you are just looking at the 00.

What happens is that although 2000 is greater than 1999, if you are using YY, then you are comparing using only the 99 and 00, and because 99 is greater than zero, the code will behave as if the year 2000 is *before* the year 1999.

This will mean that at the stroke of midnight on January 1st, 2000, suddenly programs will start to act as if tomorrow is before yesterday.

No one was quite sure how many programs were out there and what they would do if suddenly tomorrow was before yesterday. The theory was that there were countless programs that had code that read:

IF **DATE2 < DATE1** THEN **DESTROY_WORLD**

Okay, maybe it wasn't that simple, but Y2K really was all about dates inside the code of programs that would trigger something to happen when today suddenly was before yesterday.

Section 6: The Processor is just a Machine

A processor is a machine. I know that technically we could consider our brains to also be a type of machine - a bio-electro-chemical machine - but a processor is a machine the way your car, or a radio is a machine. It is an electronic machine made up of wires and transistors. It is completely man made, there is nothing 'bio' about it.

It is also not natural, it did not evolve, and it was not inevitable that it would be invented. Processors are not based on any law of nature that all the advanced technological species in the universe will use to build their own. They are human invented machines.

And they are machines with somewhat simple functions.

I would be lying if I said that the internal workings of processors were simple, but what a processor does, the operations it performs, are pretty simple. Think about driving a car. The internal workings of a car are complicated, and yet what a car does and what we have to do to make it do what it does are very simple:

I don't know how many parts there are between the steering wheel in your hands and the tires on the road, but all you do is turn the steering wheel and the tires turn. It's a complicated mechanism but a simple operation.

Or the radio, you hit a single button to go to your favorite station. That's just one button, but you know there is more than one thing going on inside that radio.

Processors work just like other machines and by pushing the right buttons, the stuff that processors do will happen. The big difference with processors is that all the buttons are on the inside and can only be pushed by entering codes that indicate which buttons (switches) to push.

This is kind of a very important point - the codes that we send the processors are doing nothing more than setting a bunch of switches inside the processor, and the result is exactly what is supposed to happen when those sets of switches are set in a particular way, just the same as setting switches on any (mindless) machine.

We may call the codes we send the processor 'instructions', but they are just another pattern of bits which are to the processor just a list of bits to set, which are just a bunch of electronic switches to turn to zero or one.

How about a little thought exercise?

Pretend there is a machine with rows of toggle switches and a row of lights and a big green button that says 'GO'. The way this machine works is that the lights on the machine will light up in a pattern that depends on how the switches are set. So, if you switch all the toggle switches on or off and hit the 'GO' button the lights will light up in a pattern.

As you set the different pattern of switches and hit 'GO' you will notice that it results in patterns of lights that may not be obvious as to why. Sometimes flipping a single switch will cause all the lights to change, and sometimes switching all the switches will cause only one light to change.

If you keep doing this over and over you will notice that the patterns of lights are not random - that the exact same pattern of switches will always give you the exact same pattern of lights.

This machine works that way because it is wired to work that way, and that is how the machine called 'the processor' works - it is wired to result in patterns based on how rows of switches are set, and the exact same pattern of switches will result in the exact same pattern of lights.

There are of course, some important differences between a processor and the machine I had you imagine - with the biggest difference being that the results are in patterns of other switches instead of lights, also there are many more switches and therefore many, many, more combinations, and instead of a big green button to tell it to 'GO' there is a clock that sends out pulses that tell it 'now, now, now,..., but otherwise this is how a processor works.

The reason it is so important to picture the processor as just a machine that is wired to react to switches in ways that are a function of how it is wired is because *a processor is just a machine that is wired to react to switches in ways that are a function of how it is wired*.

It is nothing more than that.

Really.

Of course, the processor is not wired to result in patterns that don't serve any purpose, they could, but they would not be very useful if they did. So, the processor is wired to do particular things, and the switches are wired to set up what the processors do.

Some of the switches are used for the numbers that you want to do something with (parameters, input data, that kind of thing), some of the switches are used for the operation that you want to do with those numbers (instructions), and when the processor gets the signal to 'GO'. It just does what it is wired to do, it gives a result based on the switches.

This might lead many people reading this to wonder - can a machine that just puts out a pattern of bits as a result of how switches are set really do things like let Alexa talk or create CGI characters in movies or any of the other fantastic stuff computers now do.

The answer is - yes, they can, by doing lots of little things very fast.

Section 7: Processors Do Little Things Very Fast

One of the reasons that software is so important is that processors are not wired to do the stuff that people want computers to do. The only way to make them do anything useful is by combining a whole lot of these little operations, the ones that set the switches.

You might be surprised at how little and simple the operations are. For example, just take adding two numbers. Processors can add two numbers in one operation only if the two numbers being added and the result are all small enough numbers to fit into the number of bits the processor works with at one time. Otherwise there would be a carry and it would take more than one operation.

If the processor works with 8 bits, all three numbers in the addition equation had to be 255 or less. To add larger numbers it would take combining several operations.

There are even things that seem like simple little operations that are actually combinations of even smaller even simpler operations that occur inside the processor. One of these is division.

Most processors have a division operation. But in terms of the circuits that do division, it is not actually done by dividing two numbers into each other. You may remember from back in elementary school that division is sometimes thought of as repeated subtraction. When you say 'how many times' does one number go into another number, you are asking how many times can I subtract one number from the other.

The way division is done inside a processor is to subtract the number being divided over and over by the number it is being divided by until it is too small to divide anymore, and the answer (the dividend) is the count of how many times it can be subtracted by, and whatever is left over is the remainder.

This works perfectly with one exception - do you also remember from elementary school that one special number that you can't divide into any other number?

That's right - the number zero.

This led to a really bad problem with early computers: the dreaded 'DIVIDE BY ZERO'!!!!

In the past if someone accidently divided a number by zero the processor would subtract zero from the number over and over again until it couldn't subtract zero anymore, which can take somewhere around forever.

This was one of the most insidious examples of what is known as an infinite loop, because if the computer could run forever, the computer would keep subtracting zero forever.

This was something the processor would do on its own without any additional instructions, and because they really only do one thing at a time, it would devote all it's time to doing this one thing until it was done that one operation which was of course - NEVER.

The effect was to cause the computer to hang and the only way to stop it was to have the computer be shut down and restarted.

Many young programmers had to hang their heads in shame and explain to their boss that the reason the company's computer system was down and all those data entry people weren't doing anything is that they accidently let some divisor somewhere in their program go to zero.

Whole computer systems were brought to their knees this way.

But don't worry - this was such a problem that all modern processors have extra built-in circuitry that detect whether a program is trying to divide by zero, and have code to interrupt the infinite loop. However, on some calculators, if you divide by zero, you will discover you have to turn it off and on to get it to work again.

What I was getting at before I went off on my divide by zero tangent is that the things processors do are very small and simple. Even though division is a separate operation, it is a compound operation and requires that several simple operations be combined to accomplish.

That's how simple the processor operations are, division is not simple enough to be a single operation.

Even though the processor is only doing simple operations, it does them very fast. Between the time someone would divide by zero and someone shuts down the computer a number could have been subtracted by zero millions or even billions of times, even in the old slow big processors of the past.

This is all possible because electronic switches are very fast. The speed comes from the ability of electrical signals to go from one state to the other in very short periods of time.

One day, way back in the 1980s, I was standing behind an electrical engineer as he was looking at an oscilloscope to check out the timing of a signal, as he looked at the scope he commented "that's 40 nanoseconds - that's a really long time", I laughed and told him: "no, 40 nanoseconds is not a long time". But I got the point - to an electrical engineer, trying to get the signals to be correct, 40 nanoseconds was a long time, when the signal should have only been 5 nanoseconds.

In case you never deal with nanoseconds – a nanosecond is a billionth of a second.

Electrical signals can go from one state to another very quickly. Inside processors the change is measured in billionths of a second (nanoseconds) or even trillionths of a second (picoseconds). Inside a processor the internal switches can react to the 'GO' signal so quickly that they can complete one operation and then move on to the next operation in millionths or even billionths of a second.

As I have mentioned, processors don't do very much in a single operation, and they don't have to. When you can do a million or even a billion things in a single second, each thing you do doesn't have to be very much.

Section 8: Processor Operations - What They Do

Warning: I'm going to talk about code:

In order to explain what processors do, I need to mention the code we write to tell them to do stuff. This is not the code that most people are used to, most of it is not complete English words, but two, three, and four-letter mnemonics, and they will seem strange - almost like I am talking in well... ah ...code. But don't worry, this is code you will probably never be required to translate or decode, even if you end up working with computers.

What are the kinds of things processors do during each operation?

For those of us who used to write assembly language code, which is a type of code that is turned directly into direct processor instructions also known as machine language, we used the same few commands over and over again for practically everything.

By the way, you do not need to remember any of the code I am discussing, I just wanted to show what kind of things are done when programming a processor directly. It shows what processors actually do.

The most commonly used instructions and their mnemonics are:

move	MOV
and	AND
or	OR
exclusive or	XOR
not	NOT
compare	CMP
jump	JMP
jump if equal	JE
jump if zero	JZ
jump if not zero	JNZ
jump if not equal	JNE
jump if less than	JL
jump if greater than	JG
increment	INC
decrement	DEC
add	ADD
subtract	SUB
push on the stack	PUSH
pop off the stack	POP
call a routine	CALL
return from a routine	RET
input from a port	IN
output to a port	OUT

These are not all the available operations, but with these alone, you could program everything. You might be even be able to drop a couple more from this list and still accomplish what you need by combining some of the remaining ones.

Although very few people ever write this type of code anymore, the machine code that this code generates has not gone away. In fact, all the code that everybody anywhere writes at some point ends up at the processor as machine code instructions, which, by the way, are all just numbers in the form of bit patterns. Unlike the commands of the programming languages that most people are used to, these numbers are the instructions that the processor actually executes.

By far the most commonly used operation is the first one listed: move (MOV) which does not actually move anything, it copies bit patterns from one location to another.

In describing what a processor does I said that numbers go in, numbers are manipulated, and numbers come out. The MOV instruction is how the numbers move in and how the numbers move out.

If you want to do anything to anything with a processor, whatever it is, has to be inside the processor, and once you do something to something inside a processor, if you want the result, then you have to get it out of the processor. MOV is the instruction to get things in and out of the processor which is why MOV is so important and used so much.

A good portion of the time, the only thing the processor is doing is just moving stuff. For example, anything you see on a screen or hear from a speaker is stored somewhere as a large list of numbers. In order for these numbers to get turned into the little color dots on the screen, or vibrations from a speaker they have to be moved from where they are stored and sent to the electronic devices that turn them into colors or sound.

When you are playing music that you have stored on your phone, there are a lot of bit patterns being moved from one place to another and not much else.

With pictures it's the same thing, the data in the form of zeros and ones is stored on something and the processor moves it to a device that turns that data into points of colored light on a screen.

I want to take this moment to make a point. It doesn't matter to the processor what the data is or what it is used for, the processor could just as easily send video data to a sound device or sound data to a printer. Until the data gets to the thing that uses it, it's all just zeros and ones, which is why we can use the same commands for everything.

Of course, we use the other operations in the list, but if the operation is doing any kind of manipulation of a bit pattern, a move command is used to get it into the processor to be manipulated.

So now let's look at one of those bit-manipulating operations. We will look at 'OR'. It is kind of simple, it's a typical thing that processors do, and it is a very handy operation for twirling bits.

The way it works is: If you take two bit patterns of equal size and 'OR' one with the other, if the same bit in either pattern is a 1 then the result is a 1, the result is only 0 if the bits in both patterns are 0.

How about this – I will write it as an equation:

0000 **OR** 0000 = 0000
0001 **OR** 0000 = 0001
0000 **OR** 0001 = 0001
0001 **OR** 0001 = 0001
1010 **OR** 0101 = 1111

The reason why 'OR' is so handy is that it is a direct way to turn on bits (switch them from 0 to 1), though it would take a while to explain why we would want to turn on bits directly, just trust me – it was very useful.

Another operation that is done all the time is to compare. The mnemonic is CMP, and it is used to create conditions. It only handles numbers, and it gives whether the two numbers are equal, not equal, less than, less than or equal to, greater than, greater than or equal.

All comparable conditions in all programs come down to using numbers in particular ways and comparing two of them at a time.

Now for one last type of common operation – program control. These are operations where a program switches from one part of a program to another.

I thought I would pick on the jump-if-equal (JE) command:

JE *other_code*

Because it also lets me show how simple processors do a whole bunch of different things.

The way this command works is that if, in a previous instruction two numbers were compared (CMP), and the two numbers are equal, then the processor will jump to the label: *'other_code'*. This means that the next instruction the processor will execute will be the instruction at the part of the code pointed to by the label: *'other_code'*, otherwise, the next instruction will be the next instruction in line. These conditional jumps are almost like a switch track for computer instructions. If the condition is met, they put you on a whole new set of instructions.

What these commands allow is to make it so a program does different things depending on the conditions, which is pretty much what we write programs to do.

These four commands move (MOV), or (OR), compare (CMP), and jump if equal (JE) are not special commands, these commands are the kind of operations that processors mostly do.

Section 9: It Takes Lots of Instructions

Let's get one thing clear - machines are really stupid. They don't know how to do anything. Even the smartest computer in the world has to be instructed how to do every little thing - and I do mean every little thing. In fact, there is no such thing as a smarter computer - they are all equally stupid.

For example, to ask a human to get you a cup of coffee, all you have to say is 'hey get me a cup of coffee' and they will know how to get you a cup of coffee, they might throw it in your face for being so rude, but they will at least know how to fill the cup and bring it to you.

But if you had this very smart robot and you wanted it to get you a cup of coffee you would have to tell it EVERYTHING. 'walk twenty steps in the direction of the kitchen counter', 'stop in front of the thing with the round glass container with the dark brown liquid', 'put a cup on the surface of the counter, ...'.

And this assumes the robot has been already been programmed with the thousands of lines of code it takes to walk twenty steps or the many thousands of lines of code it needs to understand voice commands, and the thousands of lines of code and millions of bytes of stored data to be able to do the pattern recognition and match a household item like a cup.

And depending on what the robot has been programmed to do before, you might even have to give it instructions on what a cup is, and how to lift it and put it on the counter, and tell it things like 'put it on the counter with the opening facing up', and you might have to give it instructions it on what 'facing up' means.

They are that stupid.

On the other hand, if they have been instructed how to do something perfectly, no matter how difficult or complicated the task, they will do it perfectly every single time they do it. This is not because they learned it but because the way a computer is instructed to do something is with a list of instructions, and to do something perfectly over again is simply to run through the instructions again.

If the instructions are never erased, then the computer will execute them exactly the same as before and will do what they did exactly as the time before, and the time before that, and if their memory is never erased, they will never forget how to do it perfectly.

But they're still stupid.

The reason it seems like computers are doing more and more on their own is because millions of people for several decades have been writing billions of instructions in excruciating and painstaking detail to tell these machines exactly how to do all kinds of stuff on their own.

This makes it seem like computer are getting good at everything, and they are, but only those things they have been instructed to do by humans who are getting better at telling computers what to do.

Which takes lots and lots of instructions - lots and lots of code.

I was struggling to come up with an example that clearly illustrates what we go through to make things happen with computers. It can take an amazing amount of instructions to do even the simplest little thing. What can seem trivial can be unbelievably complex and require a lot of steps to accomplish.

I finally came up with the example of something that everyone who has ever used a computer does all the time and takes entirely for granted. It is also something that shows that every single little detail has to be taken into account in order to make it work. The thing I am talking about is typing on a computer keyboard.

A computer keyboard physically is nothing more than a bunch of buttons, they may all look different and have different things written on them, but they all work the same way – they each have a number. When you press the button it sends out the number of the key and a number that says the key is down (the button has been pressed). When you take your finger off the keyboard it sends out the same number and a number that says that the key is now up.

So, all that the computer gets from a keyboard is a key number and that the key is down, and a key number and that the key is up, that's it.

Here are some of the steps that are needed to handle the keyboard:

(a key is pressed....)

The key number and a number that says it is up or down are grabbed from the keyboard and saved in a couple of variables. Call them KEYNUMBER and KEYSTATE.

The KEYSTATE variable is compared to see if the key is up or down and if it is up then jump to a whole different set of instructions for when the key is up.

Then, one at a time, compare the KEYNUMBER to see if it is a special key:

Is it the SHIFT KEY? If no, the jump to check the next special key, if yes jump to the SHIFT KEY instructions.

Is it the CTRL KEY? If no, the jump to check the next special key, if yes jump to the CTRL KEY instructions.

John J. Smith

Is it the Is it the ALT KEY? If no, the jump to check the next special key, if yes jump to the ALT KEY instructions.

Is it the CAPS LOCK KEY? If no, the jump to check the next special key, if yes jump to the CAPS LOCK KEY instructions.

Is it the NUM LOCK KEY? If no, the jump to check regular keys, if yes jump to the NUM LOCK KEY instructions.

Is it greater than or equal to the first key number for a displayable character? if no jump to check for other keys

Is it less than or equal to the last number for a displayable character? If no check for other keys.

This is just a glimpse of the kind of operations and instructions it takes to just to know what key is pressed, then there is code to determine if any keys are being held down such as ALT, SHIFT, or CTRL, then there is code to determine if the NUM LOCK is on or if the CAPS LOCK is on.

Then if the key being pressed is a regular character, there is code to fetch the character and pass it to the application that needs the character, and then there is code that starts a timer so that if the key is held down, after a certain amount of time the character can be repeated.

If the keyboard has those little LEDs to indicate if the CAPS LOCK or NUM LOCK are on, there is code that turns them on.

There is also code to buffer the keys so that you can keep typing.

The point I wanted to make is that even something as simple as pressing a key on a keyboard causes a lot of code to be executed, that every little detail has to be taken care of and that it all gets done so fast that from our perspective it is instantaneous.

Section 10: The Clock

The one last thing to understand about how processors work is the clock.

Although it's called a clock, the clock is just a circuit with a vibrating crystal, and although they refer to them as 'ticks' the computer clock actually sends out tiny electric pulses or signals and sends them at a rate of millions or even billions of times a second.

The clock sends out uniform electrical pulses that are signals that says one thing to the processor over and over again: "go, go, go, go,...."

So what does the clock do? - Everything.

Processors are mostly wires and switches, the switches are controlled by electric signals and the electrical signals are determined by the switches. The switches must be all set up and ready to go before the start of each operation, so there must be a signal to the processor to indicate that the switches are all ready.

That is what the clock does, it sends the signal that tells the processor when the switches have all been set and to begin the operation.

Each time the tick from the clock reaches the processor, the processor performs another operation.

Without the ticks of the clock the processor stops, it is the thing that drives the processor, and each time the computer processor gets a pulse from the clock, all the internal electronic mechanisms move forward one step. This is what keeps processors moving forward, it is what processors reacts to, to make them do what they do.

Jargon Explanation: Processor speed

The rate that the clock chip sends the ticks to the processor is the processor speed. Hz is how many 'ticks' per second. For example when you hear that a processor's speed is something like 1.2 GHz (1.2 gigahertz). A gigahertz is a billion hertz, which is a billion ticks per second. That means the clock is sending that processor 1.2 billion 'ticks' a second, and yes, that is a billion with a 'B'.

John J. Smith

Section 11: About Multi-core Processors

Most computers that most people use have only one main processor. However, the main processor in most computers that are built today (including tablets and smartphones) have multiple 'cores'. What this means is that on the same chip are several exact duplicates of a single processor. This allows the work being done by the processor to be divided up and distributed to the different cores, so that multiple things can be done at the same time, potentially making the computer faster.

I know I have said that processors only do one thing at a time, and because each core can act as a separate processor, these multi-core processors can do as many things at one time as there are cores to handle it. But keep in mind that each core only does one thing at a time, and the things they do are the same kind of small operations that a processor with only one core does.

Also, how efficiently the software uses the additional cores varies from program to program and is never 100% efficient, so two cores will not give you twice the speed.

PART THREE: PROCESSOR + MEMORY = COMPUTER

Section 1: DA DO RAM ROM

One thing about processors is that they are not built to keep anything hanging around. Every time a new set of numbers is loaded, the previous set of numbers is lost, because inside the processor the numbers are just patterns of switches, and each new set of numbers that gets loaded changes all the switches.

This means that the instructions and parameters must come from outside the processor, and after an operation the results must be sent to outside the processor. This brings us to where the numbers come from that go into the processor and where they go to when they come out. It is a special thing you all have heard of with a simple but extremely important function - memory.

Do not think of computer memory as being anything like human memory, it does not 'remember' the same kind of things, in fact it doesn't really remember anything, it's a thing where bits are stored as either zeros or ones.

Try to picture a big board made up of a grid of small squares, and the small squares can flip over, and one side of each of these little squares is black and one side is white and whatever side, black or white is showing, it will stay that way until something flips it to the other color.

I guess I don't have to mention that the little squares are the bits in memory, and the one color is zero and the other color is one - oh well - I guess I just did.

Just like everything else digital, everything is bits, but what is so special about memory is that the bits in memory stay the way they are set until something comes along and changes them, and the thing that comes along and changes them is the processor.

We refer to what a processor does with memory as reading from and writing to memory, but this is a little misleading. What is really happening is that when a processor reads from memory, it is taking patterns of bits that are in memory and duplicating them inside itself, and when a processor is writing to memory, it is taking a pattern of bits from inside itself and copying them into memory.

Processors read and write the bits in memory in chunks. Early computers had processors that set eight bits at a time, but now a lot of processors move 32 or 64 bits at a time, and that is what it means when you hear a processor described as a 32 bit processor, that it moves 32 bits at a time.

So even though memory is a boring uniform grid of bits, it is very important because everything a processor processes - all those sets of numbers, all those zeros and ones - come from, and go into memory. Simply put, without memory, a processor would have nothing to do and it would therefore be completely useless.

There are different kinds of memory used in computers for different purposes, but of the different kinds of memory, the one that most people think of and are talking about when they talk about memory, is RAM which stands for Random Access Memory, which is memory where any location in the memory can be read from or written to at any time (at random).

So, if our big board of little squares is random access, the processor can go to any square in the grid at any time and read the bits that are there or set them. That's all it means by 'random access'.

Then there is ROM - Read Only Memory. Read only is what computer people call stuff where there's something there that can't be erased or written over. You can think of books as a non-digital form of Read Only Memory. Things like CDs and DVDs are considered Read Only Memory devices.

So, going back to our big board with the grid of little squares, if we had a ROM version, the little squares in the ROM version could only be set to black or white once and then they can never be changed.

So why do computers need ROM? - oh, I am so glad I am pretending you asked.

One of the issues with RAM is that it loses all its bits when the power is turned off. When a computer is turned back on, there would be nothing in memory for the processor to read in and do, no instructions, no parameters, just empty memory, all the little squares would have the same color showing.

Here's the problem - the processor is the only thing that can put anything into memory, but it can put things into memory only if it has instructions to put things into memory, but the processor gets all of its instructions from memory. This creates a kind of chicken and egg problem: when a computer is first turned on, how does the processor put instructions into memory without the instructions in memory to put the instructions into memory?

No, it's not a time-travel paradox, just a classic chicken-egg situation.

ROM solves the chicken and egg problem of starting up a computer. Computers come with ROM that has the instructions permanently built into it that instruct the processor to load programs into memory (RAM). When you turn on the computer it uses the instructions from the ROM to load programs into RAM - problem solved.

By the way, if you ever wondered why turning a computer off and then on again makes most problems go away, it is because when you turn it off all the bits in RAM get erased, and when you turn it back on it runs from instructions in ROM that are always there and always the same.

Over the years there have been several other kinds of memory invented that do not lose their bits when the power is turned off and can also be changed. This makes it possible to update the instructions a computer uses to start up. But in terms of how it is used to start the computer they act the same as ROM.

What it really means to have a kilobyte, megabyte, or gigabyte of memory:

Because the word kilobyte means a thousand bytes you would expect that a kilobyte would be 1,000 bytes. But there is a quirk in the way we count bytes. The number being used to count is not in decimal, but in terms of a power of 2. So, a kilobyte is considered to be 1024 bytes because 1024 is the closest power of 2 to 1000 (1024 is 2 to the tenth power. 1000 is 10 to the third power.).

Therefore, a kilobyte is 1024 bytes, a megabyte is 1024 X 1024 = 1,048,576 bytes, and a gigabyte is 1024 X 1024 X 1024 = 1,073,741,824 bytes.

Section 2: Accessing at Random

The number of bits in memory is huge, - well at least to us humans, and the number keeps growing, there are lots of places to put things in memory. Which brings me to one of the most wonderful things about memory. Each and every one of those places in memory where you can put things has a unique address, a number that points to exactly where they are, and using this address the processor can get to any of these places any time it wants, and it takes no more time for the processor to get to the first location than to the last location, or any location in between.

Random access means precisely what the words mean - the processor can access any location in memory at any time in any order - at random.

Memory is numbered from 0 to the highest amount of memory there is, one memory location at a time. The numbers for the locations of memory are literally referred to as addresses and a processor can get at any particular location in memory by just using the address alone and here's what makes that so powerful - memory addresses can be used in programs.

In fact, memory addresses are one of the most frequently used numbers there are in programs. This is because memory is where all the really useful stuff is kept, everything from the programs themselves to all the data used in the programs, pictures, parameters, variables, well, …everything.

If you have written programs you will notice that everything has a name. But by the time an instruction gets to the processor it's the address of the names that is being used. Names are just a way for us humans to not have to keep track of addresses. When the program is turned into machine language all the names are gone and replaced with the addresses. To us humans what our variables and parameters are called is important, but to the computer it only matters where in memory they are.

This allows all kinds of stuff to happen. Most data come in blocks. For example, a picture is just a bunch of numbers all in a row. When a program wants to change the picture on the screen all it has to do is switch the address from the start of the block of numbers for the picture being displayed to the start of the block of numbers of the picture to be displayed.

In some ways the ability to switch from one block of data to another, which can be anything: names, pictures, sound bites, even code. It is one of the most powerful tools a programmer has.

Section 3: Processor & Memory Sitting in a Tree

We are surrounded by what we call 'smart' devices. All these smart devices have one thing in common, well actually two, they all contain both a processor and memory, and when you combine a processor and memory what you get is a computer.

In the 1980s there was a children's toy called a Speak N' Spell. It was like a calculator for spelling words (you can still buy them online), and it was a 'smart toy', which means it had a processor and memory. This was a time when there was still a Soviet Union, and for national security reasons it was illegal to sell the Speak N' Spell to the Soviet Union because it was on the list of restricted technologies.

At the time there were jokes about this restriction based on the idea that the Speak N' Spell was a toy that did one thing and one thing only, but this toy had a processor and memory, this toy was a computer, and like all computers it could be programmed for anything that computers could be programmed for, which includes things like guidance systems for missiles or control systems for fighter jets.

There is a misconception about computers that the processor is responsible for the specific functions that the computer does. I have seen several science-fiction movies where the plot involves a special processor that when it is put into things, it makes those things smart and able do things like talk and think and take over the world.

The funny thing is that what makes processors so powerful, is not because they do special things, but because they do not do special things. What makes processors so powerful is their versatility, their ability to be programmed to do anything.

What really makes things smart is a combination of the programming and information being used by the program and the programs and all the information are in memory. Processors may execute the instructions, but they are getting their instructions and information from memory, and that is where they are putting all the results.

So if you want a computer or a smart device - you need both a processor and memory.

Section 4: Why More Memory Is Always Better

In some ways, the only way to really understand how a computer works is to understand how memory is used. The funny thing about calling it memory, is that its greatest property is not its ability to 'remember' which is the ability to hold on to information. The greatest thing about memory is that anything in memory, every instruction, every instruction, every parameter, can be replaced over and over again (very fast) without limit.

Essentially computer memory is a big scratchpad. The processor does all the work, but it can't keep a hold of anything. The processor can't even hold on to the code that instructs it, the processor must go to memory to get everything it uses, and it must put the result of everything it does back into memory or it will be lost.

Try to picture it this way:

Think of the processor as the ultimate power tool. It has the power to change anything into anything else. It can turn empty space into a house, and change the house into a dog, and then it can change the dog into ten thousand bananas and then back into empty space again. But instead of this power tool doing all these things with real matter in the real universe, this tool does these things in a special virtual universe called memory, with virtual matter called bits.

Looked at it in this way, bits in memory are the raw materials for everything that computers do, and what those raw materials are made of are billions of tiny little things that the processor can turn from zero to one and from one to zero.

The memory contains all the stuff that processors work with. All of it. We have gotten used to computers doing more and more and the single biggest reason that they can do more and more is that they have more and more memory.

Processors still do much of the same things they have always done, they have a few new tricks usually for speeding things up but in terms of basic functionality they kind of work the same. They are many times faster than they were, but processors still just manipulate bits in memory. But the amount of memory, the number of bits that processors have available to manipulate has grown exponentially.

The first IBM PC I bought came with 16 Kilobytes of memory. The laptop I am writing this book on has 16 Gigabytes of memory, that is a million times more memory (a million times!!) which means that the processor has a million times more stuff to work with.

The kinds of stuff that memory gets used for is basically everything. Take for example video games. The diehard gamers who play their games on computers know that they need lots of memory to play the great games because the great games have lots of stuff.

They have high resolution video which is a lot of stuff. All the characters, weapons, and vehicles are all stuff, how the parts of the game move and react is all stuff. Every sound in the game is stuff, and of course, all the programming is stuff. And all that stuff is kept in memory.

And memory is not just for games, though games do use one heck of a lot of memory, it's needed for all of the things we do with computers. The whole concept of buffering is about getting stuff into memory. A buffer is just a regular chunk of memory that has been dedicated for collecting video information.

As we push our computers to do more and more things keep in mind that the main task for the processor is to be fast, but what really makes a computer able to do all those things is giving the processor as much memory that is needed to work with to do those things.

Memory is where all the stuff in computers goes, that's why there is never enough memory, because let's face it - we always want more stuff.

Section 5: Peripherals - Things That Do Stuff

Although I said that a processor plus memory is a computer, that combination alone is not very useful. Although I hesitate to compare a computer to a brain, in this case it might be helpful in order to understand the role that is played by all of the things we attach to computers.

If our brains were not attached to things that give it information such as our senses no information would be going into our brains. If our brains were not attached to all those parts of our bodies that we use to do things, our brains would have absolutely nothing they could do. Theoretically our brains could still do all that thinking stuff, but they would have nothing to think about and nothing to do with the thoughts, so it would render that super powerful organ in our skulls absolutely useless.

This is the one way in which the brain-computer analogy holds true. There have to be things that computers attach to that bring them information, and things that they are attached to that use that information for them to be useful.

There are all kinds of things we attach to computers. Some are very simple and do nothing more than take simple electric signals and turn them into digital numbers, things like keyboards and computer mice.

We attach things to computers sometimes with wires, sometimes as boards plugged into the computer motherboard and sometimes as circuits that are actually part of the motherboard.

In some ways these are the workhorses of the digital world and responsible for most of what we really like about computers.

As you have been reading through this book, if you have wondered how can a bunch of zeros and ones being flipped by a processor in memory do all those things that computers do, it has a lot to do with these things we attach to computers.

Some of these things are computers themselves. Sound cards are a good example. They have a special processor called a DSP which stands for a Digital Signal Processor. The DSP in a sound card is almost exclusively dedicated to taking the information, the zeros and ones that make up the sound data, and sending it to a chip which converts it to electrical signals to send to amplifiers to make sound.

Although there have been many advances in processors in the last 50 years, some of the most fantastic advances in digital technology has been in the creation of new and better things to attach to the computers.

The variety of these devices is a tremendous, it includes keyboards, game controllers, scanners, network communication cards, sound cards, video adapters, servo motor controllers, sensors, thermometers, gyroscopes, and the list goes on.

What these devices have in common is the way they communicate with a computer. Because no matter what they do, whether they move things, display things, print things, control things, detect things, whether it involves sending data into a computer, or receiving data from a computer, or both, they are communicating using bits - zeros and ones.

So to answer the question how can a bunch of zeros and ones being flipped by a processor in memory do all those things that computers do, it is because there are lots of devices that have been invented that take those bits that are sent to them by computers and convert them into the real world stuff that they do.

PART FOUR: DIGITIZING THE UNIVERSE

Section 1: Analog to Digital by Keyboard

Computers didn't really become useful until we started to use them for things that regular people do. It's all well and good to have them figure out the exact trajectory of a spacecraft, and to determine how long to burn the retro rockets, but that's not exactly what the general public is in to.

They really became useful when we started to use them for things like keeping track of business and word processing and baseball statistics and things like that. But those things required an initial step - digitizing stuff.

Basically, we can't do anything with computers unless we turn what we want to work with into digital data. That's right, we had to turn words and business records, and dates and dollars into - you guessed it - zeros and ones.

There are lots of ways to digitize things - almost as many as there are types of things to digitize, but I am going to start with what is probably the slowest and most widely-used analog to digital conversion device there is - the keyboard.

Most people don't think of a keyboard as an analog-to-digital conversion device but that is exactly what it is.

John J. Smith

Practically every letter of every word that is on every computer and computer network in the world, including the Internet, has been turned into digital data by having some human somewhere type it in. This is a very simple process, type a key, a number is sent that is stored as a pattern of zeros and ones.

Section 2: Digitizing Sound

Of course, character-based data is only a fraction of what is now on computers. We have sound, and pictures, and those groups of pictures called video, and maps, and brain scans and, well frankly, everything and the way these items get digitized is very different than the way we digitize characters. The way most things get digitized is by taking a series of measurements of the thing and saving the measurements as numbers.

For example, we digitize the position of our hands with trackballs and mouses (is plural of a computer mouse - mice or mouses? Will someone please answer this important question!!!) that measure distance by how far and in which direction a ball rolls.

Some things we want to digitize change so fast that we have to take lots of measurements very fast in order to digitize them accurately, or at least accurately enough to be useful. The best example of this is sound. The main thing we do with sound is listen to it, and therefore it must be measured fast enough to reproduce the sound in the way our brains are used to hearing it.

Sound is made up of vibrations that disturb the air and excite certain structures in our ears. If you think about vibrations as something that goes up and down, which is exactly what you get if you measure them, the speed of these vibrations is how fast they go up and down.

Thanks to an old analog device called the microphone, measuring sound is kind of easy. Inside microphones sound hits something that moves, and using things like magnets, that movement is turned into an electrical current. This makes a microphone a sound-to-electricity converter.

In order to digitize sound the computer takes measurements of the electric current coming from the microphone and saves the measurements as numbers. So here comes the tricky part - how fast do the measurements need to be taken?

Back when the CD was being developed, the two trade-offs were how fast to measure sound and how big did CDs need to be to hold all those measurements.

Sound is measured in vibrations per second and here is the thing about measuring vibrations. The number of times you measure is called the sample rate and the sample rate must be fast enough to measure both the rise and fall of the sound wave.

The math here is somewhat simple, if something is rising and falling once a second then you have to measure it twice a second to see it go both up and down. Most humans can hear notes as low as 24 vibrations per second all the way up to 22,000 vibrations per second. So, in order to have enough samples to measure up to 22,000 vibrations a second, the sound must be sampled 44,000 times a second. The number originally used for CDs was slightly larger: 44,100.

So, 44,100 times a second the electrical signal coming from the microphone is measured, and all these measurements are saved as series of numbers, which just like everything else that is digitized, the numbers are saved as zeros and ones (are you sick of me saying that yet?).

But it turns out that some people have very sensitive ears and 44,100 is not enough samples to accurately map out some very high-pitched sounds that these people hear as too sharp and piercing. It has now become a common practice in recording studios and other professional applications to use higher sample rates such as 48,000, 96,000, or even higher.

Section 3: Digitizing the rest of the Universe

Us humans are not done digitizing stuff, in fact we are just getting started. I used sound as an example because it is something that most people understand, but many things are digitized in the same way as sound - a series of measurements taken to create a mathematical model of what is being digitized. This can be temperature, wind, the ocean tides, heart beats, or even the dimensions of solid objects.

It doesn't matter what it is, the most accurate and useful way to digitize for most of the things in the analog (real) world is to measure it. Because measurements create a mathematical model of the thing being measured, and a mathematical model can saved and worked with as numbers, and those numbers can be represented as zeros, and ones.

The really great part is that some of the best work in digital electronics has been in the hardware, software, and processes used for measuring things. Like the way they attach balls to people and use cameras to essentially measure their movements to use in movies.

Or the way they can put a box around home plate and measure whether a pitch is in the strike zone with a very high level of accuracy.

Giving Away the Trick

PART FIVE: SPEED AND CHEAP BITS

Section 1: The illusion of being Instantaneous

Up until now I have been discussing how things work and how we do them. I have mentioned that things are fast, but now I want to explain how it is speed that really accounts for everything we have come to expect from computers.

Computers don't really do most of what they appear to do in the way they appear to do them. They do nothing all at once, nothing immediately, and nothing instantaneously. Everything they do is after the fact, is done in many steps, and takes an amount of time to complete and yet they seem to do everything they do immediately, instantaneously and all at once. This is an illusion. It is done by having things happen so fast that we cannot see them happen, the functions of our senses and our brains are just too slow to detect all that happens when computer functions happen.

When I talked about the instructions it takes for typing on a keyboard I didn't even get into all the additional steps it takes to get the character to show up on the screen, and yet it seems to be instantaneous as if there is direct mechanical connection between the key and the character printing mechanism, so as soon as you push a key down you see a character show up.

John J. Smith

Nothing happens on a computer unless the list of instructions that make it happen is executed, and instructions take time, to execute, they just don't take very much time. When things take a few millionths of a second we are not going to really notice.

Section 2: Pretending to Multi-task

Most people do multiple things at a time on their computers. They type things in the foreground as they are printing in the background and waiting on something to load. A smartphone on its own does multiple things all the same time - it is acting like a phone, a camera and a computer all at the same time.

Playing a video game can involve multiple separate functions such as getting commands from the controller and updating the video and sound, along with player movements, and score keeping, all at the same time. It would be understandable for someone to believe that computers do multiple things at the same time, even though I have repeatedly said that processors only do one thing at a time.

The way most computers multitask is by not multitasking at all, but by everything taking turns one-at-a-time. This technique which very effectively creates the illusion of multitasking is called time-slicing.

This is where random access memory becomes an extremely powerful tool. Each slice has its own block of memory with its own instructions, parameters, variables and data, and when it is time to go to the next slice all the processor has to do is jump to the block of memory for the next slice. In this way computers can run multiple programs all at once.

The way it works is that each slice of each program gets a certain amount of time to do what it has to do and then when the chunk of time is up the next slice gets a turn. This keeps going around and around and everything keeps moving forward a little bit at a time, but so fast that everything seems to move forward all at once and all at the same time.

Before I go on, I want to mention that although individual processors only do one thing at a time, some computer systems have multiple processors either in the form of processors with special functions such as video cards and audio cards, or in the form of multiple processor cores, or even actual duplicate processors. Although these other processors do allow computers to do real multitasking, the main purpose for them is to help the computer to run faster. When it comes to the main functions it is still only one processor feeding them data and calling all the shots.

Section 3: Real Time

I am pretty sure you have heard the term real-time, and you probably have a good idea of what it is. The best way to think of real-time is in terms of 'now'. To most people - and you would not be wrong - real-time means now is now, that what is happening at this very moment is what is actually happening at this very moment.

But for those of us who have worked with what is referred to as 'real-time processing', real-time has a very special meaning, and that meaning also concerns the issue of 'now'.

Computers never do anything on their own, ever. There must be something that happens to cause them to do something, a stimulus of some sort that they can react to. And anything they do, any reaction they have, means that a bunch of lines of code have to be executed. With some things, sometimes lots of lines of code have to execute - for example - video games. So that what seems to be happening now is actually happening after some code has executed, in other words something that seems to be happening now, is not actually happening exactly now - it just seems that way.

If you push down on one end of a seesaw the other end goes up at the same time, but if this was a computer-driven seesaw and you pushed down on one end, the other end would only go up after some code executed that instructed it to go up, it would just seem to go up at the same time.

Real-time processing is therefore writing code that executes in such a small amount of time that people do not perceive any difference between when they did something and when the reaction to the thing they did occurs. Human perception is very fast, but not fast enough to tell the difference between now and after a few lines of code have executed. So if you hear the term real-time, what it means to the people writing code is how much can they do - how many lines of code can they get away with - before we can perceive any delay.

So, thanks to computers getting faster and faster, more and more code can be executed and still seems to be taking no time at all. That's one of the main reasons that games have gotten so much better, the processors are fast enough to execute a lot of instructions and are able to do a lot before anyone notices.

Section 4: Small Fast Cheap Bits

Did you ever hear of Moore's Law?

There was this guy named Gordon Moore who was one of the founders of Intel. He made an observation that became something between a prediction and marching orders for his industry about how many transistors can be packed onto silicone chips. The reason why this is important is that transistors give us bits and it also gives us more complex computer logic, which gives us faster processors.

His original statement was that the number would double every year and after a decade he revised his statement to say that the number would double every two years. The main effect of Moore's Law has been that about every 18 months the size of memory doubles in amount but the size of the chips stays the same.

There are several practical results of Moore's Law. The first one is economical. As the amount of available memory per chip was doubling, the cost per chip was staying relatively the same or even dropping, which meant the price per bit was being cut in half every couple of years. When I said my laptop has a million times more memory than came with my first PC, it, of course, didn't cost me a million times more, in fact the cost of my laptop was cheaper, and that isn't even adjusted for inflation.

Another practical result was size. If when I bought that original PC I wanted 16 Gb of memory I would have needed a million chips, plus all the wiring and air conditioning. Now 16 Gb is on a single chip.

But one of the best results of Moore's Law is that as the transistors got smaller, and the wires between them got smaller, memory and processors got faster.

So, with the emergence of much more memory and much faster computers all kind of things that were not even possible have now become the way we do things. In other words - with speed and cheap bits we can do incredible things with hardware, like build small powerful computers we call smartphones, and all those really cool tricks we can do with them.

Section 5: Speed gives us Full-Motion Video

Years ago, when computers were first finding their way into people's lives, they didn't do much of the things they do now. It was because of speed, but it wasn't a matter of degree, they were simply not fast enough for it to be even possible to do some things at all.

Probably the clearest example of this is full motion video like TV or movies.

Most people understand that video is just a series of pictures with slight changes from one picture to the next that are displayed one after another very quickly. Even though they are called frames, they are just single still images. When movies were being invented they discovered that it takes changing the picture a minimal amount of times per second in order to fool the brains of most people into thinking they were seeing smooth motion instead of a flickering series of still pictures. That number is about 24.

So the challenge to do full motion video on a computer was to put up 24 pictures per second onto the screen.

Digital pictures are, of course, just a bunch of numbers (zeros and ones), with each number being a color dot on the screen. How many dots are on the screen will determine how many numbers there are per picture. For this example I am going to use the numbers for HDTV which is 1920 columns of dots across and 1080 rows of dots up and down. That means it takes 2,073,600 individual color numbers to be moved through memory and put on the screen for each frame. So, if we multiply that by 24 - the minimal number of frames per second we need for the appearance of smooth motion - we get about 50 million color dots that must be displayed on the screen per second.

50 million sounds like a big number (and I guess it is) but when a processor is doing several billion operations a second, it will barely break a sweat (especially since processors don't sweat), but for the earliest personal computers which used to only do several million operations per second, that isn't just a big number - it's an impossibly big number. For those machines it was not just difficult - it was completely impossible to do full motion video.

Section 6: Speed Brings You Virtual Reality

I was going to discuss Virtual Reality in the last part of the book where I discuss some of the more elaborate tricks we do, but virtual reality isn't really one specific thing, and it requires speed, lots and lots of speed, so instead of getting too deep into how it is done, I wanted to show how it isn't even possible without ridiculous amounts of processor speed.

Virtual Reality is a collection of things that work together to fool a person's senses into thinking the stuff being presented to them is real. In order to do that and be convincing, what you send to a person's senses has to match the expectations of the person's brain especially with regard to motion and time.

The basic challenge of virtual reality is keeping up with what a person's brain expects to happen due to a lifetime of experience in the real world.

The biggest challenge of all is matching what our brains expect to see when we turn our heads. To begin with, our brains are really used to seeing what we are looking at change at the same rate as we turn our heads. When we look left, we expect to see what is on the left of us, as soon as we turn left.

When we turn our heads wearing the VR headset, if the video in the headset, what we are seeing, takes even the slightest amount of time to catch up with where we are looking - if there is even the slightest amount of lag time - it can either ruin the illusion of reality or even worse, it can be disorienting and even cause motion sickness.

But computers don't read minds, so until we actually start to turn our heads the computer does not know when we will start to turn or which direction or how fast we will turn it. The computer must wait until we start to turn before it can know what pictures to put in front of our eyes in order to simulate what we are looking at.

VR is a classic real-time application, and practically speaking, real-time processing comes down to how many lines of code can execute before things starts to lag.

But it takes a lot of lines of code to figure out the direction and speed we are turning and even more code to calculate what we are looking at and even more code to display the correct video in front of the person's eyes. So until it was possible to execute all the code that it takes to do all those steps and have no perceivable lag time, virtual reality wasn't really possible.

Section 7: Speed Makes Computers Seem Smart

I just want to point out that computers are not actually getting smarter. I know it seems like they are, but they work the same way as they did fifty years ago. But there are lots of good reasons why it seems like they are getting smarter.

The programs are certainly getting more sophisticated and they are able to include much more data from many more sources when they do things and they can do many more calculations in a shorter period of time and with AI techniques and machine learning, they have started to use data that they collect themselves and process on their own.

With all these things working together it lets computers do things the same or better than humans and usually many times faster. It would only be natural to assume that they are actually getting smarter, but it is an illusion created by computers getting faster.

Those things computers do well, they do perfectly. They have perfect memories, they never make a math mistake, their analysis using binary logic is flawless. If they have been programmed to do something, they will do it again and again without even the slightest deviation.

But this has always been the case. In every area that computers are better than humans they have always been better than humans. The reason we think that computers are getting smarter is really because they are getting faster.

Example one: Chess

There was a point in the ancient times of the 1980s when the big question was - will computers become smart enough to beat a chess master at chess. It was thought that chess masters were some of the smartest people in the world, and that if computers could beat them that would mean that computers have become smarter than the smartest people.

Well there are now computers that can beat anyone at chess. So that must mean they are really smart and out-thinking the smartest people - well not exactly.

Chess is a bunch of simple calculations and a humongous bunch of options, conditions and consequences - ('if their pawn is there and my knight is here and if I move my queen six places over there, ...').

So playing chess is figuring out what you can do and what your opponent can do in response. Every time you make a move in chess it changes the conditions and creates a whole new set of options for your opponent and every time your opponent moves it changes the conditions and creates a whole new set of options for you.

Coming up with the best next move in chess is figuring out the best consequences of every possible next move and all possible consequences of all the possible consequences of all the possible next moves of your opponent - or something like that.

The problem is, that for each move ahead that you consider, the number of possible options and consequences are multiplied, and pretty soon there are so many possible options and possible consequences that no human can really think of them all. But a computer can, in fact if it's programmed to do so it can figure all possible options and consequences.

Doing all those calculations takes time, even for a computer. Earlier systems that did not win every time did not figure out all that many moves ahead, because the more moves ahead the computer was programmed to figure out the longer it would take before it could come up with a next move. Human intuition, and the experience of a chess master was much more efficient.

But with faster computers not only can they figure out many more moves ahead than any human possibly can, they do it in such a short period of time that it seems like the computer just knows what next move to make. It makes them seem smarter even though a slow computer could calculate the same exact moves, and win just as many games, with the only difference being it would take much longer.

Example two: Human-sounding Voice Simulation

If somebody says that they are going to talk like a robot, you know that what they mean is a slow stiff monotone voice where every letter is pronounced a little too clearly. This is the way the first voice simulations sounded like. We didn't really think of that 'robot voice' as coming from something that was all that smart.

There were several ways of creating the robot voice, but it was done by stringing together the sounds of the letters in the word or whole words, kind of the way a printer strings together the letters and words it is going to print.

Then came the early GPS devices, and then the virtual assistants like Siri and Alexa, which are just another type of robot with a simulated voice, where the voice is smooth and multi-toned and sounds like the way people talk. The way that this is done requires a whole lot more speed to accomplish than the old monotone robot voice.

The generation of the voice has to include things like how the word is being used, where in the sentence it occurs, whether it is part of a question or a statement, plus a whole lot of more subtle things that people do when they speak.

For each of those things that are part of the way people speak and the tone they use in the context they are speaking requires algorithms and all of the sound data that goes with it.

By putting it all together in a way that makes the answers sharp and snappy, the illusion of a smart knowledgeable person is created.

So even though it is not the result of a computer actually being smarter, it is easy to think of a machine that talks like a person as so much smarter than one that talks like a robot, especially when they have all the answers.

Example three: A little About Artificial Intelligence

I know that computers really do seem to be getting smarter, but that's just because by building on top of everything that came before, their programming has become very sophisticated and their capabilities are expanding rapidly.

An argument could be made that software is getting smarter, but software is lines of code, just lists of instructions that tell the computer exactly what to do. It seems like a contradiction to say that computers are getting smarter because people are getting better at telling them what to do.

But what about artificial intelligence?

Artificial Intelligence is not really a specific thing that you can point to and say – 'that's artificial intelligence'. The best way to describe artificial intelligence is that it is a collection of techniques and algorithms that altogether make computers act smarter.

When people think about artificial intelligence, they typically are thinking about computers acting more like they have human intelligence. That computers can think, know, learn and understand. Some people believe this is leading to computers becoming conscious and self-aware.

But what we call artificial intelligence is software, it is a list of instructions, and lists of instructions cannot think, know, learn, or understand, and lists of instructions will never become conscious or self-aware.

But lines of code on a fast-enough computer can simulate thinking, knowing, learning, understanding, consciousness, and self-awareness, as anyone who has interacted with an AI personal assistant can attest to.

Computer programs have lots of conditional statements. These are commonly referred to as 'if - then' statements, as in: 'IF such and such condition exists THEN do such and such'. This allows programs to react to conditions. The more conditions that a computer is programmed to react to the more variety of conditions it can handle.

Being computers, however, the only conditions that computers actually react to are data, and the more

118

different kinds of data that the computer reacts to, the less that humans need to intervene and the more you can let computers do things on their own, and the smarter and independent they seem.

If this is taken one step further and the computer is programmed to respond to new conditions by saving the data of the circumstances of the new conditions, and then add that data to the list of conditions it can react to, it will appear to learn and appear to get even smarter.

Then if the computer is programmed to react to conditions in a human-like way, accounting for all the subtleties and variations of human behavior, you will start to have computers that can handle many conditions - maybe more than most people, while acting like humans do. This will make the computer appear to be learning and knowing and understanding things like a human, except smarter, but at the heart of this behavior is not a thinking brain, but a very fast processor and enough memory to do it.

Example 4: Big Data

Let's take this a little further, to the concept of big data, or should I write it BIG DATA.

Us humans collect a lot of data on computers. It wasn't decided one day that we would collect it, it's just that we put things into computers and computers never forget, then computers just doing what computers do started to generate and collect data themselves.

The amount of data is exploding.

Every day on every stock exchange, every share of stock in every company that is sold is saved as data. Every weather event that is measured is collected, every piece of medical data from every patient is collected. Every business transaction, every piece of data on every product that is bought or sold, is collected.

Basically, everything that is put, recorded or generated on every computer everywhere is collected, and that means thanks to the Internet, everything that happens on the Internet is also collected.

There is even this stuff called metadata, which is data about the data. For example, the metadata for a phone call can include: the two phone numbers, when the call started, how long it lasted, and thanks to the GPS features in smartphones it can even include the latitude and longitude of each of the phones.

All of this data can tell us something but going through it all is an impossible task for a human, or even groups of humans, or even for extremely large groups of humans. But a computer can go through it very fast, and groups of computers can go through it even faster and all kinds of things are being found out from these computer-based analyses.

And the most important reason that this is happening and growing is speed. It takes a lot of processing power to crunch billions and billions of pieces of data and doing something a thousand times faster means the difference between days and years.

From all this data the computers are discovering all kinds of correlations, all kinds of associations and all kinds of solutions to all kinds of problems, though most of those solutions are coming from finding things inside big bunches of data that some smart human came up with that works.

The promise of being able to go through data and finding answers and solutions is one of the most exciting areas of what is considered artificial intelligence and it is not because the computers are getting smarter but because they are getting faster.

PART SIX: A FEW GOOD TRICKS

Preface:

I decided I was going to limit the big tricks that I talk about to just a few. This whole book has been about how we do all of the tricks we do with computers, and these are just some examples of pulling together the things discussed in this book to create things that are nothing like they seem to be in the same way that magicians use levers, and wires, and trap doors, and smoke and mirrors to create things that are not what they seem to be.

But the main reason for limiting it to just a few is that I want to finish this book in my lifetime and there are already way too many things we can do with computers to even talk about a tiny portion of them, besides, this technology is actually in it's infancy, and it's impossible to imagine all of the things that humans will think up to do with it in the future.

We have become very used to things that not only could not be done before or did not exist before, but were not even conceived of before, so I have some rather high expectations for the future.

The limits on what new tricks we can think of is the human imagination, which, so far, has been somewhat limitless, and with software, when we invent things, we don't even have to worry about the laws of physics.

Section 1: First Tricks - Programming Languages

We have reached the point in time where it is just accepted that people can communicate with computers using spoken language. This is, of course, a trick. Computers don't really understand what you are saying, they don't even understand what *they* are saying. Specifically, processors do not work with language at all, they don't even understand the code that is written to instruct them.

The earliest digital computers were programmed in a direct wiring kind of way. Or by flipping physical switches to set up the operations, and the code being entered were binary bit patterns, - they were entered as zeros and ones. This was not even slightly practical, but it got things started.

The instructions that are in the form of bit setting (zeros and ones), which us humans would write as numbers, is called machine language because that is really what the machine works with, they don't even work with code. Code is just an easier way for us humans to write up lists of machine language instructions without having to type them out one bit at a time as zeros and ones.

But even this code which is called assembly language must be fed into a program called an assembler to be turned into the zeros and ones of machine language.

Giving Away the Trick

The programming languages that most people are familiar with are what are considered 'higher level languages'.

Somewhere along the line programming languages became categorized by their levels and for some reason, it was decided that the lowest level languages were the ones closest to machine language, with machine language being the lowest level language, and assembly language being the lowest level language for humans.

Not that knowing any of this is important, but it lets me get to what is probably the best trick of all, the one that has paid off in practically everything that we do with computers and much more to come, and that is: higher level languages.

The section on how it takes a lot of code to do anything was based on the fact that it takes a lot of assembly language code to do anything because it takes a lot of machine language instructions to do anything, but most people, no matter how technical their job is, never have to learn the code at this level.

The languages that give computers instructions using code that is easier to understand are called higher level languages, and they really are one of the best tricks of all, and the best part is that each higher-level language can be used to make even higher-level languages.

The way it works is this - everything that you do with a computer takes multiple processor-level instructions. If you have a list of instructions that does one particular thing — for example, inputting a character from a keyboard. All the lines of code it takes to bring in a character typed on a keyboard can be bunched together and given a name.

For example, most higher-level languages have an INPUT statement of some kind, and all you have to do to run all that keyboard input code to load a character would be the single simple statement:

INPUT

Another example of this is the 'PRINT' statement found in almost every high-level language. Processors do not print. They send bytes of data to a printer. The arrangement of these bytes of data is controlled by instructions sent to the processor, and, depending on how much the print statement in the language automatically does for you, it can be thousands of lines of machine language instructions that need to be executed to get the correctly formatted data sent to the printer to print, but all the code you have to write is 'PRINT' and name the thing that you want to print.

So, consider the building process, if each statement in a language is a program that runs when you write that statement, then groups of statements in *that* language can be grouped together to become a statement in an even higher-level language.

For example, you could group statements that extract information from a database, sort it in a particular manner and combine them with a series of print statements to create a higher language statement that you call 'REPORT'. Then all you would have to do to get a complete, properly formatted report is write one statement:

REPORT *name_of_thing_to_report*

The key to higher level languages and the building process is that each line of high-level code causes groups of lines of code in a lower level language to execute, which causes groups of lines of code in an even lower level language to execute until what is actually being executed is many machine language instructions. It's kind of a code pyramid.

So when you have extremely high-level languages such as when you ask a Siri or Alexa a question, by the time you get the answer it could be millions of different machine language instructions have been executed all based on a single statement such as:

'Alexa weather'

Before I leave this section, I want to add a point about high level languages that may not be obvious, which is that they are part of the man-made evolution of the machines. Computers do not evolve on their own, but they do have a form of evolution. The more accurate way of saying it is that we evolve them, and we do it by building higher level languages out of the languages in the next layer down.

I talk about this unnatural evolution later in the book.

Section 2: Searching for Answers

Probably one of the most useful tricks that computers do is give answers to questions. Long before Google existed computers were used to find things, all kinds of things. There are large collections of information called databases, and all you have to do is ask a question about something in the database and up pops an answer.

This has progressed so that now we have these things we can actually ask in plain spoken language all kinds of questions and get all kinds of answers and the answers are spoken back to us in plain spoken language. If these things were people, with how fast we get the answers, we would think that they knew a whole lot of stuff, that they know practically everything. But it's a trick. Computers literally do not know anything.

What computers do is go through lists of words very fast and find words that match the words in the question, but even this is a trick - words, which are strings of characters, are just strings of numbers, each number representing a letter in the language. When they are looking for a word, they are really comparing numbers. In order to find a word that begins with the letter A they go through lists of strings of numbers and compare the first number in each string of numbers to the number for the letter A. Then go to the next number in the string for the next letter, and so on.

John J. Smith

The reason they find things so quickly is because they can compare numbers so quickly. Each single letter comparison is a single processor operation and they can do millions or even billions of these a second. When Siri or Alexa answer a question, in that slight pause between when you ask the question and you get the answer, the words you say have been turned into string of letters, which are really strings of numbers and then they do a search by comparing these strings of numbers to the strings of numbers in huge databases.

By doing all these steps one at a time so fast it seems instantaneous, it is easy to be fooled into thinking that the thing you just asked a question of, actually knows the answers and can tell you what the answers are.

Section 3: Seeing What's There

There is a whole area of digital technology involved in what is called pattern recognition. This is a really great trick, and depending how it is used, it can be part of some incredible applications, everything from automatic surgery to finding bad guys from surveillance video and pictures.

It can also make computers seem really smart by letting them interact with the world around them by just looking around by themselves. But it is a trick and it probably does not work like you might think it does.

Pattern recognition is considered one of the more important techniques in AI. We have gotten used to computers doing things like retinal scans, and thumbprint scans and facial recognition and many people have started to think that computers can know what they are looking at and understand the difference between things as if they are smart enough now to tell one object from another.

But the reality is a bit more mundane, and not so very intelligent, and as with everything else involves doing small simple things one at a time at a very rapid pace.

It's a trick.

To explain how it is actually done, the example I'll start with is the simplest of all pattern recognition tasks - recognizing a black dot on a white piece of paper.

We first take a blank piece of paper and put a tiny black dot in the middle.

And let's first see how the human does -

We hold up the paper in front of one of us humans and ask what do you see? Almost immediately the human answers - 'there's a dot in the middle of the paper'.

So how did the human see that dot? How should I know? - I'm not a neurophysiologist.

But us humans have this weird ability to take in the full field of view and tell at a glance what we are seeing.

Ok so let's try the machine.

We have a computer that has speech recognition software, and a camera. We hold the piece of paper in front of the camera and ask the same question - what do you see? Almost immediately it answers: 'there is a single black dot in the center of a white field'.

So how did the machine do it - did it just look at the paper, take in the full field of view and tell at a glance what it saw?

Nope, not even close - remember it's a trick. Here are the steps:

First step is to have the camera take a digital picture.

That puts the number for each color into the memory of the computer. If it's an HD picture, there are 1920 X 1080 points and therefore a little more than 2 million color numbers in memory and assuming that the paper is uniform and white, pretty much every one of those color numbers is the same - the number for white.

The next step is to take each color number for each point, one at a time, and compare it. That's right, it means going through each and every one of those 2,0073,600 color values that make up the digital picture in memory to determine what color each and every point is.

So the computer will do the same number comparison 2,0073,599 times: what color is point 1 - white, what color is point 2 - white, what color is point 3 -white,... on and on until it has gone through all the numbers and if and when it comes across the number for black, it saves the location, and then continues on until it has compared every last point.

The only way a computer can 'see' that black dot is to go through the color value of each and every point, one at a time, to calculate if there are any points with the color number for black. It cannot make assumptions, it cannot guess, there are no shortcuts.

Grabbing a number from memory and comparing it are very small operations and when processors can do millions or even billions of operations a second, it doesn't take very long to go through 2 million comparisons - just a tiny fraction of a second. Which makes it seem like the computer can do what us humans do - just glance and know. But they can't that's why it's a trick.

Section 4: Facial Recognition

I'll admit that a single dot on the center of a white piece of paper is not much of a pattern for a computer to recognize, but I wanted to first warm you up to the process before I got into the math that the computer has to do in order to recognize other more complex patterns, such as what might seem the most difficult (it's not) pattern recognition task of all - facial recognition.

I know it might seem really cool that your phone recognizes you and can then address you by name, but it really doesn't recognize you in the sense that it knows what you look like. Your dog is better at knowing what you look like than a computer (of course your dog knows what you smell like better than what you look like).

Computers have no concept of a face. They do not see anything the way we see things, they are very bad about what things look like, but they are great at math, and when it comes to faces, they are really good at calculating the mathematical differences with the layout of people's faces.

It starts with a digital, or a series of digital pictures. Then going through each point in the picture one by one, a layout of the color and shading differences are mapped out in memory. Not every feature is part of the map, and the map does not include every detail of the features it maps.

There are features on our faces that we all have that are mathematically similar, and located in mathematically similar locations relative to each other, features like our eyes, nose, mouth, and ears.

With these features, not only are the features themselves different from person to person, but how they are positioned on our face relative to each other is different from person to person, and these differences can be measured.

Here's the cool part - the differences can be very small, so small that us humans just can't really see them. We just don't have the ability to see at a glance if one person's eyes are 1/2 millimeter wider apart than someone else's, but a machine can. Depending on how close and clear the picture of the face is, these measurements can be so accurate that a face can be recognized very close to absolute certainty in a fraction of a second.

So if you have grown closer to your phone because it recognizes you and calls you by name, it's probably a good idea to remember that it's a trick and all you are to your phone is a bunch of calculations that come out the same as the last time it seemed to recognize you.

Section 5: Talking with Machines

I have to admit that I think being able to talk to machines is one of the best tricks of all. There are certainly a lot of things computers do that are extremely cool and mind-blowing, like really good virtual reality, or the CGI they use in movies, but being able to just say something in regular language and have them respond correctly is great, it fools the mind into thinking computers are getting more like people, especially when they reply in very human-like voices.

People actually thank them and refer to them as he or she as if they have the gender of the voice. I try my best to always refer to these talking machines as 'it' and try never to be polite as I would to a real person, but every so often I forget it's a machine and say 'she' and throw a totally unnecessary 'thanks' it's way.

How very embarrassing.

So, what does it take to make this happen? Massive amounts of data, fast processors, millions of lines of code, and some really heavy-duty math.

But let me back up a little bit. I have talked about pattern recognition, and for most people they might be thinking of visible patterns, which is understandable considering how much we depend on what we see, but computers don't see anything, and they don't work with anything but numbers.

Really when you get down to it, any time a computer determines what a series of things is, even if there are only two things in the series, that is pattern recognition, and the patterns are always mathematical patterns, patterns of numbers.

The only way that a computer can recognize anything is to somehow get it into a series of numbers and compare the numbers to other series of numbers. This is true of words, pictures, motions, and measurements, and it is true of sound.

But speech is not just any sound. It can be one of the most complex sounds there are. When turned into a series of numbers it is an extremely complex mathematical series. It is not just a pattern, but a pattern of patterns of patterns.

and when trying to decipher the pattern, it is never an exact match. You could have the most well-trained speaker saying the same word over and over again and none of the patterns would match, which is why this trick is so amazing.

What the algorithms do is match the very complex patterns that make up the words we say into what are close enough matches. It's not perfect, but it's pretty good and getting better every day. I figure in a few years these programs will be able to match the words of an intoxicated person with a thick accent and a speech impediment.

PART SEVEN: SOFTWARE, THE REAL MAGIC

Section 1: Software – a real superpower

As someone who has been developing software for as long as I have, I have a very expansive view of what we can do with it, namely – we can pretty much do anything.

I sometimes joke that it's a superpower.

Consider this - in a few years practically every machine on Earth will be controlled by software, even your toaster, and most of those machines will be attached to the Internet. This means that if someone knows how, they can control any machine in the world from anywhere in the world.

I started to realize just how much power a person who knows how to make these things work has when I started to read about hackers using the cameras on people's laptops to look around their houses and spy on them – from anywhere in the world.

This is a clever idea, but it is not an especially difficult hack, but how is being able to look around someone else's house from the other side of the world not a superpower? Even Superman can't do that.

The other part of my joke is that it is also a very slow superpower. The machines are fast, but the power is with people instructing them and it all takes time to do. Threatening someone with your software superpower would be something like: "I will destroy you and your family and everyone you know…in six to seven months … with testing and debugging".

But really consider how much control software has over people. Everything that everybody looks at on every screen and display, every sound you hear from any speaker anywhere, every motion from every machine is the result of lines of code being executed.

Software makes everything happen.

What is Software? It can include many things, but I prefer the simplest definition – it is anything that is not hardware or content. Hardware being, well, hardware, and content being all that stuff we consume with our brains: the stuff to read, listen to, or watch.

Software is programs, code, computer instructions, algorithms. The tools and mechanisms for doing the tricks.

Section 2: Programming What Can Be Programmed

When magicians design tricks, they have a specific goal – they want to make it appear as if something very specific happens. Things like sawing a woman in half, pulling a rabbit out of a hat, or making the Statue of Liberty disappear.

In order to do this, they break down each part of a trick into a series of individual events, and then invent ways to do each of those events. Then when these things are done together, usually in a very specific sequence, 'as if by magic' whatever is supposed to happen - happens.

Building a program is exactly the same as building a magic trick. Whatever you want the program to do has to be broken down into a series of individual events and the programmer has to invent a way to make each of these events happen.

You probably have heard the term algorithm. Well, algorithms are those little inventions. They are a way of doing something involving pieces of code that do specific things as part of a program, they are virtual machines. They are the little mechanisms, the trap doors and wires that the tricks are built with.

If something that needs to be done in a particular way can be broken down into a series of steps and those steps can be turned into a list of specific instructions, then that thing can be programmed.

So, we can reduce what can be programmed to a simple rule-of-thumb: anything that can be done the same way more than once can be programmed. Because if something can be done the same way more than once then each of the steps that are required to do it can be turned into an instruction, and the list of those instructions is the program.

This can be anything.

It doesn't matter if a process or procedure is complicated, or how many complex interacting conditions it has, as long as there is a right way to do each little step, then that process or procedure can be programmed.

This is how we build our tricks. We figure out how humans, or nature, or the laws of physics cause things to happen, break them down into steps, and write instructions to do the steps. This can apply to everything from sharpening a pencil to brain surgery.

If computers are instructed to do each of those things perfectly, or at least as good as the humans that instructed them can do them, then computers will do that thing and most combinations of those things perfectly or as good as the humans who instructed them can do them.

Giving Away the Trick

Section 3: What Can't Be Programed

There is a lot speculation about the future of artificial intelligence. We have gotten very used to our machines acting like they know what they are doing, and continually knowing how to do more. This has led to the expectation that they will eventually be able to do everything that humans do. That they will eventually become conscious and self-aware and then...

OH NO!! THE ROBOTS ARE TAKING OVER THE WORLD!!!

Many people think that artificial intelligence will eventually lead to conscious self-aware machines that will become smart enough to program themselves to become even smarter.

This has led to the belief and extreme anxiety that artificial intelligence will soon be smarter than our slow biological brains and that these AI entities will become so pleased with themselves and so disdainful of us humans that they will decide they don't need us anymore (except maybe to float us in goo for electricity).

So, about this whole 'the machines getting smarter and taking over the world' thing – I'll start with the bad news for us humans - in the many ways that computers are smart, they are already way smarter than us. They have perfect memories, perfect analytic skills, they can calculate anything with perfect accuracy, and do it faster than in a blink of the eye. Every piece of information that humans have ever generated is sitting on some computer storage thing and of course it is available to the machines instantly any time they want it.

If they can do something we can do - and they already do much of what we can do - they will do it correctly every time. If you put them to work, they don't get tired or hungry or grouchy and they never sleep or get sick. In so many ways they are way superior to us humans.

However, there is also good news for us humans.

The good news is that there are some things that digital computers cannot do because there are things that cannot be programmed, now or ever.

What are those things I am talking about?

Let's start with a couple of big ones: knowing and understanding.

Computers do not know anything, not in the way that people do. They know things in the way that a library does. Libraries have vast amounts of information but the building itself doesn't know anything. All the information is written in books and is only useful when some human reads it.

With computers, instead of the characters in the book being printed on paper, they are arrangements of electrons on disk drives and other digital storage devices, but that information is only useful when some human reads it or when a synthesized voice tells the information to a human.

Because computers can access the information very quickly it does seem like they know the information, but it is just a trick of matching characters in a word to a block of information on a hard drive somewhere.

As for actual understanding, there is not one piece of data that means anything different than any other piece of data to a computer. It literally (and yes, I am literally using that word correctly) is all just zeros and ones. We program computers to arrange the zeros and ones in a way that is meaningful to us, as text, or pictures, or sound, but that does not make it meaningful to the computer. To the computer everything is just bits to switch and move.

Most people have heard the expression 'machine learning'. The techniques involved in machine learning are used all the time, and it does seem that the machines are really learning, like when programs start to learn our preferences and learn all about us and what we like to do.

I know I'll probably disappoint some of you and reassure others by saying this, but computers do not really learn. Computers are programmed to use data and often that data is used as parameters in a program. Machine learning typically involves the computers collecting data from a situation as it occurs, and then adding that data to the pile of data it has and uses, so that the next time it encounters a similar situation, that new data it saved can be looked up and used in some way.

Even in this situation the computer does not understand the data it is collecting and using, it just uses it the way the algorithms are programmed to use it.

Also, in the 'cannot be programmed' category are two very big things that go together, these are: consciousness and self-awareness.

It doesn't matter how fast or how much memory you have. It does not matter how many computers you connect to each other. There is just no way for digital computers to ever be conscious or self-aware.

I have heard several people argue that because we are machines and we are conscious and self-aware it is possible for a machine to be conscious and self-aware. This might be true, but a) we do not really know what makes us conscious or self-aware, or even how consciousness works, b) we are not digital, and c) my consciousness is asking why am I discussing this anyway?

Computers will only do what they are programmed to do and when I say only - I really do mean *only*. This means that everything you have ever seen a computer do has lines of code making it do it, which leads to a simple, maybe even obvious point - there is no possible way for lines of code to become conscious. There is no possible combination of instructions that results in actual thought.

Consciousness simply cannot be programmed.

I have really struggled to find a way to explain why it cannot happen, but the best explanation I can come up is to state that because there is no conceivable way to make it happen, it cannot happen.

But if you really are not convinced think of it this way. Our brains are extremely complex things, and one of the functions they have is to be conscious. So assuming that a brain is subject to the laws of physics, it is safe to assume that the brain, as one of the few things that we know of, that is both conscious and self-aware, that consciousness can only come from the combination of our complex brain hardware and complex brain processes.

How could it be possible for something that has no common physical hardware and has no common internal or external processes to suddenly and spontaneously end up with a common function – consciousness?

You know, in the alchemy days, they thought they could change lead into gold because in many ways lead acted just like gold. Conscious, self-aware computers is the alchemy of our time.

To think that digital computers will become conscious and self-aware is no less ridiculous than thinking if you put four wheels and a steering wheel on a cardboard box it will drive like a Ferrari.

Giving Away the Trick

Okay, now that I got that out of my system … oh wait a minute…

Just a quick thing to add – if something can't be conscious, it can't be self-aware.

Period.

Which brings me to that thing that would be really big and scary if it really could happen. This is the concept that is the basis for all of the AI-run-amuck doomsday scenarios. It is the concept of computers becoming smart enough to program themselves to become smarter.

Sorry, ain't gonna happen.

Information does not make us smarter or more intelligent. It is how we understand and use that information that makes us more intelligent. The way that computers use information is by way of algorithms and algorithms are created by people, because, unlike computers, we actually understand the information we work with.

Yes, there is software being created that can create other algorithms and I know this has many people very worried that the computers will get very good at creating algorithms and then with all the information in the world that they have at their disposal, that they will start to program themselves to be smarter than us.

So, let me break it to you here – this cannot happen.

It isn't because the machines cannot be programmed to be smarter, it's because humans cannot program the machines to program themselves to be smarter. It's kind of a philosophical/mathematical thing.

In order for a computer to program itself to become smarter, a human or humans would need to create a program to do that. They would have to write a list of instructions that instructs the computer to generate its own new lists of instructions that are more sophisticated ('smarter') than the list of instructions that the computer is using.

(…was it the chicken or the egg…)

(… can God create a rock so big that even God can't lift it?)

Or stated in another, more confusing, circular way: it would take a program that is smarter than the human programmer who programmed it to be able to program programs that are smarter than themselves.

I am quite certain that it is not possible to write programs that are smarter than yourself, but if you believe that it is possible, I have a perpetual motion machine I'd like to sell you.

But enough of this, I had another reason for talking about what can't be programmed.

Section 4: Faking What Can't Be Programmed

Although computers are really useful, they are not especially warm and cuddly, for that I prefer to hang out with people. But for some reason, people seem to want to have their computers act more like people. But the challenge to do that is that most of those things that make us uniquely human cannot be programmed.

The things like emotions and empathy and morality, and free will, are functions of that big thing we cannot program - a conscious mind - and without a conscious mind, there can't be any of those things.

But this is where the fun begins, because - just because they cannot be programmed doesn't mean we can't fake them.

Besides, who's going to know?

It is those things that cannot be programmed that are the basis for the best tricks of all, because although computers cannot do these things, computers can be programmed to make it seem like they can do those things.

These are real magic tricks, because what is a magic trick anyway, but a way of faking the impossible so convincingly that people believe it is real.

One of the most powerful parts of any program are the conditionals. These are those things that make programs able to handle different situations, contexts, and yes, conditions. They are sometimes referred to as 'if – then' statements, or 'if tests', and what they are, are the points in a program where a decision is made to use one list of instructions or another depending on a condition or a set of conditions.

The reason it is these conditionals that make programs so useful, and powerful and complex, is because the conditions are whatever the software developer wants them to be and they can be sequenced and combined any way you want.

'if G occurs before H but not after J and if A and B but not C or D then do Z'

There can be huge trees of conditional code where, by the time a program checks for the last condition in the tree there could be thousands, tens of thousands, or more possibilities. The more conditions that a program handles, the more sophisticated the program is and the smarter that program seems to be.

Which brings me to how to fake what can't be programmed.

How we judge the world around us is based on what we expect to happen, based on what we know. We have built-in expectations of how someone should behave and what kind of responses we think we should get. We impose our own set of human conditionals on everything:

- If he doesn't get here on time, then I'm leaving.
- If she can answer the question correctly, then she's hired
- If my dog barks, then he wants to go out.

Humans react or behave in ways that indicate a response to conditions. We cry when something happens to make us sad, we hold out our hands when someone says they want to give us something, we give answers when we are asked a question.

The stuff in our brains, like consciousness, emotions, empathy, and thinking, that drive our reactions to conditions are just that - in our brains - and are not visible, the only thing visible to others are the external signs of our reactions to those conditions. The tears, the movements of our bodies, the words that come out of our mouths are the only things that other people are aware of.

The trick to making computers seem to do things that they really cannot do is to make their visible and audible reactions the same as the visible and audio parts of human reactions and program them for enough conditions and combinations of conditions that it seems they are reacting in the way a human is expected to react in similar situations or conditions.

Example 1: Consciousness

Without going into what consciousness is, the question is - how do we know if someone else is conscious? We know that we, ourselves are conscious in a 'I think therefore I am' kind-of-way. But how do we know that someone else is conscious? Well, we don't really, but we infer it from how they react to us. We talk to them, and they respond, we respond to their response, and they respond to our response to their response, and so on.

The personal assistants like Siri and Alexa are programmed to respond to a request or comment and because the response is usually a correct one, delivered in a way that a conscious human would respond, our brains immediately start to adjust to feeling that we interacting with a conscious person.

On more than one occasion I have found myself saying 'thanks' to Alexa for giving me the weather forecast (please don't tell anyone I told you that).

So, if computers could conduct a human-like back-and-forth exchange, or have a full conversation, and if their responses were relevant and seemed to come from a conscious person, it would be very hard to tell if they were conscious or not.

Example 2: Self Awareness

Then let's extend this to self-awareness.

Once you have a program that is programmed to give relevant answers as part of a full conversation, to make it seem self-aware you would program it to give answers with references to themselves. For example, you might program a robot to point out its own characteristics, to say things that make it seem like it is aware of its own strengths and weaknesses.

The personal assistants are already programmed to answer questions using the pronoun 'I'. That little word alone, spoken in the correct way in the correct context, is a major contributor to the illusion of self-awareness.

It's very convincing. It triggers that thing in our brains that makes us think we are talking to someone, that causes us to be polite.

So, just like consciousness, if the responses were seeming to come from an awareness of self, it might be very difficult and maybe impossible to know for sure that the responses were not from a self-aware entity.

Examples 3+: That Other Human Stuff

I just wanted to give some mention to empathy, emotions, pain, ethics, morality, and other human things and how we could approach faking them.

I, of course, will use an easy example – the emotion anger.

Anger is not always logical in humans, much of the time people get angry for really bad reasons, really stupid reasons, and sometimes for no obvious reason whatsoever.

Think of how easy it would be to make a program seem to get angry like a human being would.

For example, you could put a counting function in Alexa or Siri that counts the number of times a particular question gets asked over again. Then program Alexa so that on the fourth or fifth time it gets asked the same question, to give a response that sounds annoyed and angry.

"Alexa, what is the weather today"

'THE WEATHER AGAIN! – YOU AND YOUR WEATHER! – WHY DON'T YOU EVER ASK ME HOW I AM DOING?'

If it was a physical robot you might have its face turn red, have fake veins pop out, cross its arms and change the volume and tone of its voice.

This is the approach to fake these human sorts of things that can't be programmed. Just figure out all the little things that humans do when they experience that thing, mimic the visible and audible parts of the human reaction, and then program the correct conditions for when to give the relevant response.

Abracadabra – watch my robot get angry at stupid questions!

Section 5: Unnatural Selection

The reason that this section is in the part of the book about the trick to create magic with software is that the way that computers evolve is through software.

Computers have not changed very much. Computers are pretty much just processors, memory, and storage and they pretty much work the way they always did. The basic things they did is what they still do, and the code that ran on computers fifty years ago will work just as well on a smartphone.

This is a good thing.

If computers changed in any fundamental way then you would have to start over to write the instructions to make them function, but because they do not change in any fundamental way all those basic things that we count on every computer to have will be part of all the new computers.

We don't change the road, so the wheel does not have to be reinvented.

But before anyone jumps to conclusions, I thought I would mention that if you consider evolution to be a natural process – then computers do not really evolve, because they never change by natural means. They never change in any way on their own, and they never start being able to do things that that they did not do already.

The way they evolve is through changes in software – new algorithms, new uses for old algorithms and new features. But what makes this an evolution is that everything is an extension of what already exists, and everything is built on top of what has already been built before.

There was a time when each company had its own software that was built in-house, and yet even then, we tried to do as little wheel reinvention as possible. When we started to create new programs we would start by borrowing from ourselves and others in the company.

Sometimes we didn't borrow code - just the idea, because just hearing about an idea could be enough to let you create your own version of that idea, so even direct access to the code was unnecessary for software to benefit from prior developments.

This has caused an explosion in functionality with computers. A new set of parameters here, a new algorithm there, and add some graphics and abracadabra some new function or a whole new program now exists.

With the Internet connecting all these computers, all the computers are evolving at once. Functionality shows up years after you brought that old computer home just by having software updates get installed online while you sleep.

What this means is that once a feature gets accepted somewhere, that feature shows up everywhere. There was a time when they didn't have spreadsheets, or word processors, but now they all do, It used to be that computers didn't understand spoken words, now they do.

Because we usually do not have to wait for a new generation of computers, this is a much faster form of evolution than the natural kind, and the reason why computers are evolving so quickly.

There is even the equivalent of Natural Selection. If you think of a new feature or program as a mutation, then if that mutation is successful, then all the computers will have that new function, if it is not successful, it might just die off. But in reality, we hate to throw anything out, so it is more likely that the feature is sitting disabled in the program and kept around to be used later for something completely different.

PART EIGHT: THE ULTIMATE TRICK – FAKE PEOPLE

Making fake people will not be the coolest thing we ever do with computers. There are things already invented that are far cooler than that. But as tricks go – it is the ultimate magic, and we are not there yet.

In order to do this trick, we will need to mimic thousands of subtle and not-so-subtle actions, and motions, and sequences, and interactions. We have to do these things using machines that cannot really do any of the underlying brain functions that cause all these things in real people.

We have to make them seem to think, know, learn, understand, and emote when they are completely incapable of thinking, knowing, learning, understanding, and emoting.

And there is this one thing that guarantees we won't ever be able to complete our fake humans - but I'll get to that later.

We have to give them all the external signs of consciousness, when they are not conscious in the least.

We have to give them facial expressions and body language, that comes from our emotions, when they do not emote.

We have to make them look, sound, feel, and even smell organic, when they are not organic.

But in spite of the challenges, we are making great progress, and it sure looks like we will have artificial people in our midst.

For example – we have human voice simulation that sounds like a person.

The pleasant voice with the perfect accent on my old GPS in my car sounded stiff when compared to the personal assistants like Siri and Alexa. When you get a human-like voice with human-like inflection, and human-like disposition, even though that disposition is unwaveringly sunny and polite (which of course, is a dead giveaway that it's not a real person), it is hard not to think you are dealing with a real person.

We have robots with facial expressions that are getting closer to human all the time.

There are 43 muscles in the human face, and we already have materials and mechanisms that mimic muscles, it's just a matter of time before there are artificial human face skeletons with all 43 muscles with the correct size shape and function that are controlled to act together exactly as a human's face muscles would.

It won't be long before there is realistic android skin.

There will be a soft, flexible material that will be heated by small tubes running warm liquids through it. Tiny sensors will be built in to detect contact, pressure, and temperature. It will have the ability to turn any color which will be used to achieve perfect skin tone, and the ability to mimic all of the changes that occur with human skin.

The look and 'feel' of these artificial humans will be identical to the real thing. They will be the perfect assistant. Some will be made to act supportive and affectionate. Some will be made to be the perfect servants.

They will seem as human as you and I…

…except for that one thing.

There just so happens to be one thing that cannot be programmed and cannot be faked, and without that thing, we will never create perfect artificial humans.

No, it is not love. We can fake that. Humans have been faking love for thousands of years.

The thing that cannot be programmed and cannot be faked, the thing that will keep us from ever creating a robot that will act like a human in every way is:

'envelope please…'

A sense of humor.

That's right – the darn things will never get the joke. Ever.
Don't laugh, it's not funny…

... at least not to them.

About the Author

John discovered computers as a student in 1974 – it was the best toy he had ever played with. Over the next several decades he went on to develop software for a wide variety of projects including business applications, computer systems, communications, robotics, and, of course, a toy or two from time to time.

By necessity, he learned about computers the only way you could at the time: on-the-job, by asking questions, reading manuals, and making them work. A lot of trial, a lot of error.

In this book John takes his long experience and his deep and practical understanding, to tell the story of how computers really work, and how we take machines that essentially crunch numbers and make them do all the things that they now do.

www.ingramcontent.com/pod-product-compliance
Lightning Source LLC
Chambersburg PA
CBHW051241050326
40689CB00007B/1025